125 M

&
MENT

D1502952

# Fabric Almanac

# FABRIC ALMANAC

## by Marvin Klapper

SECOND EDITION

Fairchild Publications, Inc.

NEW YORK

Standard Book Number: 87005–092–3

Library of Congress Catalog Card Number: 72–132144

Printed in the United States of America

# Contents

5

# Preface

This edition of *Fabric Almanac* has been designed to give the reader a swift and accurate look at the textile industry in the decade of the '70's.

I call it a study of "fibernetics"—the language around which the industry knits and weaves its spell . . . its fibers, fabrics, trademarks, processes, definitions, and directions.

Hopefully those connected with textiles will find the book a ready reference source for a quick answer, as well as a starting point for more detailed data.

A debt of gratitude is owed to many talented people in Fairchild Publications who helped me with this work, most especially Audrey Schipper, head of the Research Department, who graciously opened her files and made available statistical data.

To the many people outside the Fairchild Company . . . and my many friends in industry . . . a note of thanks for their help. I have endeavored to use credits for organizations and other sources whenever possible.

To my friend José Martín, Allied Chemical's fashion wizard and brilliant textile colorist, a very special "Thank you" is due.

When I turned to him for help with a planned chapter on color, José most graciously offered to write it himself . . . an offer I found too irresistible to turn down.

A brilliant nature photographer as well as artist and sportsman, José supplied color slides from his own private collection —never before published—to give the chapter a unique touch that so beautifully represents his artistic talent.

Last but not least a very special hug, kiss, and thanks to my wife Blanche, who magically translated the scribbles of a tired author into beautifully typed manuscript pages—and to my daughter Sherry who supplied big doses of inspiration, love, and encouragement.

Marvin Klapper

Oceanside L.I., N.Y.
October 20, 1970

# Introduction–
# Textiles in
# the 'Seventies

**PART ONE**

As the textile industry moved into the decade of the 'Seventies it faced what many believe to be its biggest challenge . . . and opportunity. The wave of consumerism that is sweeping America is lapping at the industry's doorstep, focusing a spotlight on virtually all consumer products: their quality, ease of upkeep, durability, and even safety.

As consumerism surfaces as the most potent force in American industry the textile industry must meet the challenge. Its strategy of obsolescence must be refined, altered, and improved by adding a new dimension to its products . . . the dimension of performance. The standards of the 'Sixties will no longer suffice for the 'Seventies. Fortunately, the technology of performance is here now; only the commitment is needed, and it is growing rapidly.

The industry has at its fingertips the most sophisticated fiber production techniques ever, making possible heretofore-unheard-of blends and mixtures in the spinneret: second-, third-, even fourth-generation fibers . . . new cross-sectional profiles of filaments and yarns including bilobals, trilobals, even pentalobal fiber shapes . . . with exciting new visual, tactile, and performance characteristics.

Anti-soil finishes that repel dirt . . . durable press . . . new constructions . . . water-repellents . . . even that old bugaboo static that makes fabric cling to the wearer are being brought under control. New and better knit and woven constructions are broadening fabric appeal; finer yarn counts, lighter weight goods are adding up to a more sophisticated industry—with better products for consumers.

Not yet on the drawing boards but not too far from reality are man-made fibers that react to infrared . . . ultraviolet . . . polarized light . . . even sunlight . . . changing their colors and reflective qualities like a chameleon, perhaps opening a path to new design and fashion concepts for apparel and home textiles.

Also under investigation are new methods for altering molecules that could lead to new and better fabrics and fibers. These include ultrasonic waves, extreme temperatures, exposure to and treatment by gases, new tricks with chemistry and radiation, and other more esoteric experiments.

Simultaneously textile-machine speeds are moving up: the industry is knitting, weaving, tufting, needling, sewing faster than ever before . . . spilling out better quality goods faster. Sacred icons are being smashed in production rooms and moon-age techniques are moving in.

This trend is likely to continue in the coming decade, which will probably witness the largest and most exciting array of fibers, fabrics, and yarns ever in history.

One of the newest twists in yarn is a growing trend of texturizing to achieve new fashion dimensions. Spurred by the ravenous appetite of the fashion and home-textile industry for new and different-looking fabrics, the art of texturizing is burgeoning. This edition of *Fabric Almanac* contains many trademarks for texturized-yarn processes which now are becoming more important in the textile lexicon.

Industry observers estimate the installed capacity for texturizing yarn in the U.S. alone now exceeds some 466 million pounds—with a whopping 348 million in false-twist types—and it's growing by leaps and bounds. This development alone will reshape many concepts of both woven and knitted fabrics for a long time to come.

As an adjunct to consumerism, the question of environmental pollution also arises to challenge industry of the 'Seventies . . . and textiles are no exception. The industry is currently taking a hard look at itself and its production techniques with an eye to cleaning up abuses and restoring the natural environment, although in truth with minor exceptions textiles have never been a major violator in this regard compared with such industries as aviation or automotive.

José Martín's chapter on color is a living testimonial to the need for stronger control of environmental pollution. Taking his artistic pallette from nature . . . flowers, birds, fish, and other wildlife . . . José has long decried nature's spoilers wherever they may surface.

Harnessing nature's beauty to textile design and color has been José's life; and he is well qualified as an artist, colorist, big-game fisherman, nature photographer, conservationist to lead in this fight. Everyone has a stake in beauty. As José so aptly states, "It will remain in the eye of the beholder so long as there is something to behold."

The textile industry of course remains handmaiden to the fashion world, whose number one motivation is the desire for change. The inspirational gleam in a fashion designer's eye reverberates with lightning speed through all segments of the industry, bringing about change . . . and product excitement. The speed at which change evolves today may be simply observed. This edition of *Fabric Almanac* contains substantial additions to the basic lexicon of textiles given in the first edition, each reflecting a new concept, trademark, or definition, rather than the author's ambition to enlarge this humble work.

Keeping pace with these changes is what *Fabric Almanac's* Second Edition is all about. It is designed to give the reader a simple, easy-to-understand explanation of the words, technology, and trends of the textile world, now estimated to be the sixth largest industry in the United States.

Some idea of the size of the industry may be seen by examining its capacity. Last year, for example, it turned out about 13 billion linear yards of cotton, wool, man-made fibers, silk, and broad-woven fabrics . . . enough to circle the earth at the equator almost 200 times or reach to the moon and back 26 times. It employed almost one million people in the United States and chalked up about $213 billion sales. But the giant is not standing still: change is in the making for the decade ahead.

Communication is the key to keeping pace with this change. Never before has this need to keep current been as keen as today, for never has the industry moved as swiftly.

The technician or scientist looking for deep explanation and detailed minutiae will have to go elsewhere. But for the student, retailer, buyer, designer, teacher, technician, workroom operator, mill manager, fiber or fabric specialist, for textile management or for the consumer, *Fabric Almanac* will serve as a ready reference source . . . a place to go for a quick answer. To understand and interpret change as it occurs one must know and speak the language of textiles.

*Fabric Almanac* speaks this language simply and easily. Whether you want to find a perplexing term, a new process, a guide to industry trends, or the correct spelling of a fiber or trademark, it's our hope you can locate it all here.

If the book meets this goal, it will fulfill the purpose for which it is intended, that of being your guide to the textile world of the 'Seventies.

# Complete Fabric Glossary

## PART TWO

## A

**A.C.E.** (Allied Chemical Engineered) Trademark owned by Allied Chemical Co. for producer-textured nylon fiber for contract carpets with no-soil properties.

**Acele** Trademark owned by Du Pont for all acetate yarn products. Currently produced only in continuous filament form in bright, dull, and cycloset versions. (See FLW.)

**acetate** A manufactured fiber made from cellulose acetate. Where not less than 92% of the hydroxl groups are acetylated, the term "triacetate" may be used as a generic description of the fiber.

**Acridel** Trademark for Turbo-processed high-bulk acrylic knitting yarns for sweaters and hosiery processed by Delaine.

**Acrilan** Trademark owned by Monsanto Fibers for acrylic staple and filament fiber composed of 85% or more acrylonitrile, a liquid derivative of natural gas and air. (See Glacé.)

**Acrilan Spectran**   Trademark formerly used by Monsanto Fibers for solution-dyed staple acrylic fiber.

**acrylic**   Generic term for a manufactured fiber in which the fiber-forming substance is any long-chain synthetic polymer composed of at least 85% by weight of acrylonitrile units. Made in both filament and staple forms.

**Acrymal**   Trademark for Turbo-processed high-bulk acrylic staple yarn processed by Malina.

**Actionwear**   Merchandising trademark owned by Monsanto for producer-textured nylon hosiery yarns.

**Agilon**   Trademark owned by Deering Milliken Research Corp. for a filament synthetic stretch-yarn process that draws fiber over a hot knife-edge to impart crimp. Yarns are usually nylon, polyester, or other thermoplastic types.

**Agro**   Trademark owned by Beaunit Fibers for viscose filament yarn.

**air jet**   Technique for bulking filament yarns by exposing them to pressurized air. Most commonly used in Taslan process. (See Taslan.)

**Airloft**   Trademark owned by Celanese Fibers Co. for acetate and nylon filament carpet yarn.

**Airvel**   Trademark owned by Du Pont for British texturizing process for bulking staple fibers.

**ajour**   Openwork embroidery in lacy effects.

**Akzona**   A new American corporation made up of four companies with combined 1969 sales of $332 million. The companies are: American Enka (fibers), International Salt, Brand-Rex Co. (wire and cable), and Organon Inc. (ethical drugs). The four operating units will maintain their separate identities.

**Alana**  Trademark for high-bulk Turbo-processed Acrilan spun yarn by Templon.

**alençon**  Point lace with fine mesh ground and usually a floral design outlined with heavy thread.

**Allyn 707**  Trademark owned by Allied Chemical for nylon fiber. It's the European version of Caprolan.

**aloe lace**  Fragile lace made from aloe plant fibers from the Philippines and Italy.

**alpaca**  Hair fiber obtained from a domesticated South American hoofed mammal called an alpaca. Usually five to ten inches long, the fiber is elastic, soft, lustrous, strong. The fleece combines a soft wool-like undercoat and a stiffer outercoat. Generically, alpaca is classified for labeling purposes as wool.

**Anavor**  Trademark owned by Dow Badische Co. for polyester fiber.

**Angelrest**  Trademark owned by Celanese Fibers Co. for acetate tow for quilting.

**angora**  Hair of the angora goat, also known as *mohair*. Finest quality is *kid mohair*. Sometimes angora is obtained from the fur of the angora rabbit. Both animals are native to the Angora Province of Turkey, hence the name. The goat fiber is classified as wool. It is *not* permissible, however, to describe the hair of the angora rabbit as wool.

**Anim/8**  Trademark owned by Rohm and Haas for elastomeric fiber. Has new generic classification of Anidex fiber issued by Federal Trade Commission effective Nov. 3, 1969.

**Anso**  Trademark owned by Allied Chemical Co. for soil-reducing producer-textured modified nylon staple and filament fiber. Second-generation fiber; owes properties to polymer modification.

**antique lace**   Handmade bobbin lace of heavy thread with large, often irregular, square-knotted mesh on which designs are darned. Imitations are sometimes used in draperies.

**antique taffeta**   Crisp taffeta made of uneven or slubbed yarn, simulating types made in ancient times before silk was finely cultivated.

**Antron**   Trademark owned by Du Pont for a premium series of nylon fibers in filament, staple, or tow form. Apparel yarns have distinctive luster, dry hand, and high colorability; carpet yarns hide soil. *Antron III* is low-static yarn for intimate apparel.

**Anywhere**   Merchandising trademark of Monsanto Fibers for needle-punched indoor/outdoor carpets containing solution-dyed acrylic fiber and meeting certain specifications and standards.

**appenzell**   Fine Swiss hand-embroidery made with a button-hole stitch.

**application printing**   Also called *direct printing*. (See printing.)

**appliqué**   Motif or design made separately, then sewn or af-fixed on a cloth or garment.

**arabesque**   Highly ornamental geometrically balanced design in formalized, scrolled effects such as are used in architecture.

**Arachne**   High-speed stitchbonding process for non-woven fabrics developed in Czechoslovakia.

**Arbel**   Trademark owned by Celanese Fibers Co. for acetate staple.

**ARCT**   An abbreviation given to continuous filament stretch yarns processed on false-twist machinery manufactured by Ateliers Roannais de Constructions Textiles, licensed in the U.S. by Deering Milliken.

**2 0**

**argentan**  Lace similar to alençon but with larger designs, heavier in weight.

**Aridex**  Trademark owned by Du Pont for a water-repellent wax-emulsion finish for cotton, rayon, wool fabrics.

**Aristocrat**  Trademark owned by Beaunit Fibers for rayon filament, staple, and tow.

**armure**  Rich-looking dress or coat fabric, plain, striped, ribbed, or woven, with small fancy designs suggesting chain armor.

**Arnel**  Trademark owned by Celanese Fibers Co. for spun and filament triacetate. *Arnel Plus* is a combination of arnel and nylon in knitting yarn. May be textured and heat set.

**Astrakhan cloth**  Thick woven or knitted fabric with lofty loops or curls on the surface imitating an Astrakhan lamb pelt.

**Astroloft**  Trademark for false-twist textured filament yarns by Southern Silk. Other marks include *Astrolon* and *Astrolure*.

**Astroturf**  Trademark owned by Monsanto Fibers for recreational surfaces made of flat ribbon-pigmented nylon monofilaments. Used for baseball diamonds, tennis courts, golf greens, etc. Tailored for specific end uses and areas.

**autoclave**  Textile oven that cooks with super-heated steam and pressure to set twist or crimp in yarns.

**Avceram**  Trademark of American Viscose Division of FMC Corp. for ceramic filament fibers.

**Avicolor**  See Colorspun.

**Avicron**  Trademark owned by American Viscose Division of FMC Corp. for rayon filament yarn containing a latent crimp

21

which is activated in normal bleaching and dyeing. Another mark is *Avicrimp,* for high bulking with added crimp.

**Avisco**  Trademark owned by American Viscose Division of FMC Corp. for rayon and acetate fibers.

**Avlin**  Trademark owned by American Viscose Division of FMC for polyester filament and staple fibers.

**Avril**  Trademark owned by American Viscose Division of FMC Corp. for staple and filament cellulosic fiber with high wet strength. Use of name confined to fabrics that meet firm's quality-control standards.

**Avron**  Trademark owned by American Viscose Division of FMC Corp. for high-tenacity, low-shrinkage rayon staple fiber fabrics that meet specified quality standards.

**Ayrlyn**  Trademark owned by Rohm and Haas for nylon 6 fiber.

**Axminster**  Originally a woven carpet with a heavy pile made with a cotton or jute warp and a woolen or worsted filling. Today man-made fibers and filaments are utilized in backing and pile yarns. Term refers to method of weaving, not to appearance. Usually of many colors with pile almost always cut.

**azlon**  Federal Trade Commission's generic name for regenerated protein fibers. None is currently being manufactured in the U.S.


**B**

**bagherra**  Velvet woven or knitted with uncut loop pile.

**bainin**  Native Irish woolen homespun cloth, handwoven in the Aran Islands.

**22**

**bale**  Standard bulk package for shipping raw or processed fibers. A bale of cotton weighs 500 pounds, silk about 138 pounds.

**banding**  Woven, knitted, or braided narrow fabric, tape, or webbing.

**Banesta**  Trademark of Joseph Bancroft for fabrics of textralized polyester yarn.

**Ban-Lon**  Trademark owned by Joseph Bancroft & Sons, Inc., for a moderate stretch and bulking system applicable to any thermoplastic fiber.

**barathea**  Broken-rib semicrisp compact weave. Coarse granular effect with smooth almost satiny surface. Familiar in neckties and semicrisp dress goods.

**Barbara**  Trademark of Sauquoit for non-torque stretch yarn.

**bark cloth**  Nonwoven material made in the tropics from inner bark of trees soaked and beaten out to the required thinness, then dyed or ornamented with printed patterns. (See tapa cloth.) Also woven drapery fabric that imitates the rough effect of bark cloth.

**bark crepe**  Fabric made of twisted yarns to simulate the bark of a tree.

**barré**  A bar or stripe effect in a fabric (either intentional or otherwise) that is characterized by an apparent difference in color or shade. The effect usually extends in the filling direction.

**basket weave**  Plain weave with two or more warp and filling threads interlaced to resemble a plaited basket. Has flat look, porosity, and looseness or "give." Can be heavy or lightweight, made of any fiber.

**batik** Method of resist dyeing originating in Java. Parts of a cloth are coated with wax, which is then etched or cut to shape the design. Only the uncovered exposed parts of the cloth take the dye. The process can be repeated many times to obtain multicolored, unique patterns or designs Often has characteristic streaked effects where dye has penetrated cracks in the wax. Batik effects are often simulated in roller or screen printing.

**batiste** Named for Jean Baptiste, a French linen weaver. A sheer fabric, once mainly cotton or silk, now encompassing virtually all man-made fiber goods, if made in fine construction. Resembles nainsook, but is finer, with a lengthwise streak. Used for linings, dress goods, shirtings, corset fabrics, etc.

**battenberg** Coarse form of renaissance lace, hand or machine made from linen braid or tape and linen thread brought together to form various designs.

**bayadere** Stripes, plain or fancy, woven or printed, running crosswise in a fabric.

**B.C.F.** (bulked continuous filament yarns) Term is commonly used in carpet industry to signify textured yarn. When yarn is supplied directly by the fiber-maker it is referred to as producer textured.

**beading** Variety of insertion laces or embroidery having rows of holes through which ribbon may be laced.

**beaver cloth** Heavily fulled twill wool double cloth resembling kersey. If term is used, FTC has ruled it must be referred to as imitation beaver cloth to distinguish it from real fur.

**bedford cord** Stout, heavy fabric with raised cord or ridge running lengthwise.

**beetling** Process used in finishing linen which serves to reduce the opening between warp and filling, producing a flat effect with high degree of luster.

**belgian lace**   Pillow laces with machine-made grounds from Belgium, including Antwerp, Valenciennes, Brussels, and Mechlin lace.

**Belmora**   Trademark owned by Belmont for textured filament nylon yarn.

**Bemberg**   Trademark owned by Beaunit Fibers for cuprammonium rayon and other filament and staple fibers.

**benares**   East Indian silk-and-metal tissue fabric made in Benares, India.

**bengaline**   Warp-faced fabric with pronounced, completely covered crosswise ribs formed by coarse filling. Sometimes with rubber or spandex filling for swimsuits and girdles. Also used in women's formal coats and suits.

**Beta**   Trademark owned by Owens-Corning for ultra-fine glass filament yarn.

**bias tape**   Double or single fold of tape cut on the bias and used to bind edges.

**bicomponent fiber**   A fiber formed by spinning and joining together two different polymers . . . such as nylon and polyester . . . simultaneously from one spinneret. Sometimes called *conjugate fiber*. Differs from *biconstituent fiber,* in which two different polymers are blended together before going through the spinneret to form a single strand. FTC has amended Rule 10 of the Textile Fibers Identification Act to include manufactured fibers composed of two chemical components, called bicomponents, where the two components are combined at or prior to extrusion. The terms *matrix fibril fiber* or *matrix fiber* may be used in lieu of the designations "bicomponent" or "multicomponent" fiber.

**biconstituent fiber**   See bicomponent fiber.

**Bi-Loft** Trademark of Monsanto Fibers for a bicomponent acrylic fiber. Yarns are made by combining non-reversible crimp bicomponent with Type 16 Acrilan. Monsanto also uses the bicomponent as a core yarn in blends with Acrilan.

**binche** Durable, firm bobbin lace. Novelty-shaped mesh, interspersed with simple snowflake-like motifs. Has cloth-like texture with threads weaving in and out at right angles.

**birdseye** 1. Dobby-loom weave characterized by a diamond-shaped spot. 2. A cotton diaper cloth made in birdseye weave.

**Blanc de Blancs** Trademark owned by American Enka Corp. for improved color nylon. (Means "white of whites.")

**blanket** Wide-width cover woven in one continuous piece. Also, a fabric for sampling, showing a series of filling patterns or colors, all on the same warp.

**blanket cloth** 1. Heavyweight reversible fabric commonly woven with jacquard figures of one color on a ground of another color. Filling is thick and softspun. 2. Heavyweight overcoating fabric with soft, raised finish.

**blazer cloth** Striped flannel.

**bleeding** The loss or change of color in a fabric after washing or drycleaning. Bleeding dyes have long been associated with madras cloth from India. Domestic manufacturers have developed synthetic bleeding dyes to simulate the organic natural dyestuffs used in India.

**blend** The combination of two or more types of stape fibers and/or colors in one yarn. Blends are sometimes so intimate that it is difficult to distinguish component fibers in yarn or fabric. A highly sophisticated textile art, blending today is creating new fabric types, performance characteristics, and dyeing and finishing effects.

**block printing**   The printing of fabrics by hand using a design applied by means of a carved wooden block or linoleum-faced wood block. A slower process than roller printing or screen printing.

**blotch print**   Cloth printed by the direct method. Ground color as well as design is printed.

**Blue C**   Basic trademark used by Monsanto Fibers for all of its fibers including nylon and polyester—does not include Acrilan (acrylic), which is merchandised via the Red A.

**bobbinet**   Fine bobbin net with six-sided mesh for gowns, foundations, and dresses, and as a base for embroidered and appliquéd laces.

**Bodyfree**   Trademark of Allied Chemical Co. for new anti-static (non-shock) nylon fiber for lingerie and sleepwear fields.

**bolt**   The entire length of cloth from a loom.

**bombazine**   1. Fine English fabric in plain or twill weave, usually with silk warp and worsted filling. 2. Name used in rubberized market for a converted print cloth.

**Bonacette**   Trademark owned by Beaunit Fibers for texturized rayon yarns.

**bonding**   The joining together of two fabrics, usually a face fabric and a lining fabric of tricot, to make a double package. Fabrics can also be bonded to ultra-fine slices of foam or other materials. The science of bonding and laminating has opened new markets for knits, sheers, laces, other fragile cloths that formerly were difficult to handle on the cutting table.

**Bondyne**   Trademark owned by Greenwood Mills Inc. Applied to fabric with various percentages of natural or man-made fibers blended with prescribed amounts of Dynel modacrylic fiber.

**bonnaz**  Machinery used for rapid production of embroidery. Fabric is held taut and the needle made to move freely, outlining the design with chain stitch.

**botany**  Generic term for finest wools, worsted yarns, fabrics, used in the same sense as and interchangeably with *merino.*

**bouclé**  Fabric woven or knitted with a looped or knotted surface, usually in a spongy effect. Term is also applied to yarn with loops or curls.

**bourdon**  Cord along the edges of tapes used for ornaments in laces.

**bourré**  Best grade of silk waste.

**bourrette**  Silk yarn spun of the carded short fiber of poorer quality waste silk.

**bow and skew**  Distortion in warp and filling alignment of fabrics due to improper tensioning of fabric in weaving or finishing.

**box loom**  Loom that allows many shuttles to work. Used to weave cloth requiring more than one filling yarn, or for special colorful patterns.

**Bradford system**  A method of spinning worsted yarns, also called *English system.*

**braid**  Woven or plaited flat, round, or tubular narrow fabric for binding or trimming. Sometimes referred to as *spaghetti.*

**bretonne lace**  Net with embroidered designs of heavy thread, often colored.

**Briglo**  Trademark owned by American Enka for high-tenacity rayon filament yarn.

**broadcloth**   Closely woven fabric with very fine imbedded ribs and lustrous finish. Made in many weights, fibers, and blends. Resembles fine poplin. Worsted and woolen broadcloths have glossy finish with nap in one direction.

**broadloom**   Term refers to carpet woven or tufted wider than 54-inch widths . . . usually six-, nine-, 12-, 15-, or 18-foot widths. Term refers only to width, not quality or type. (See carpet.)

**brocade**   Rich jacquard with designs of raised figures or flowers, sometimes with contrasting surfaces, colors, gold or silver threads. Ground may be satin, twill, or a combination of weaves. Gives an embossed appearance.

**brocatelle**   A heavy cross-ribbed furniture and drapery fabric similar to brocade but with jacquard figures in high relief.

**Brunsmet**   Trademark owned by Brunswick Corp. for metallic stainless-steel filament and staple yarns. Small amounts of the fiber are blended in carpet yarns to eliminate static.

**Brussels**   Bobbin net lace heavily outlined around its design, which may be straight, as in binche, or diagonal.

**Bucaleni**   Trademark owned by Glen Raven Mills for crimped knit-de-knit bouclé polyester yarns.

**Bucaroni**   Trademark owned by Glen Raven Mills for crimped textured nylon filament yarns.

**Bulk-Eze**   Trademark of Associated Spinners for Turbo-processed yarns of high-bulk Orlon Type 42.

**bulking**   Method of altering yarns, making them fluff up. Gives soft, pleasant textures and opaque effects to both knitted and woven fabrics.

**29**

**Buonarotti** Trademark owned by Glen Raven Mills for textured yarns of Antron nylon.

**burlap** Coarse, heavy, plain woven fabric made of jute. Used for wrapping, bagging, wall covering, drapery, and clothing.

**burling** The removal from a piece of cloth of any extraneous substances such as knots, loose threads, slubs, and burs.

**burn-out** A process of printing which uses chemicals, rather than color, to burn out or dissolve away one fiber in a sized cloth. The result is a sheer lacy and heavy design. Also eyelet or other holes may be "burned out" of a cloth. Process is not too common today.

**butcher linen** Coarse homespun linen once used for aprons by French butchers. Now widely imitated in many man-made fiber fabrics.

**Byrd cloth** Trademark owned by Reeves Bros., Inc., for mercerized fine-combed ply yarn, reversible cotton twill, tightly woven.


## C

**cable twist** A yarn or rope construction in which each successive twist is in the opposite direction to the preceding twist. Defined as "s-z-s" or "z-s-z."

**Cadon** Formerly used as trademark of Monsanto for multi-lobal sparkling nylon. Now used for anti-static carpet filament nylon.

**calais val** Type of Valenciennes lace that has a round mesh like other vals but made of heavier threads and usually in wider widths.

**calendering** A process of passing cloth between rollers (or "calenders"), usually under carefully controlled heat and pressure, to produce a variety of surface textures or effects in fabric.

**calico** 1. Plain, closely woven lightweight printed cotton cloth of East Indian origin (Calcutta). 2. In England, a plain woven bleached cotton fabric heavier than muslin. Until the end of the seventeenth century all cotton goods were called calicos.

**cambric** Lightweight, sized, well-glazed inexpensive cotton or linen weave. Used mostly for pocket linings. In England, a light, fine, plain-woven linen fabric.

**camel hair** Wool-like underhair of the camel. Lustrous and extremely soft, used either by itself or combined with wool. Natural color ranges from light tan to brownish black. Classified as wool under the Wool Products Labeling Act.

**canton crepe** Thick, slightly ribbed crepe, heavier than crepe de chine, drapes beautifully. Originally made of silk in Canton, China.

**Cantrece** Trademark owned by Du Pont for bicomponent self-crimping textured nylon yarn. Formerly called Fiber H, it is used mostly for women's hosiery, pantyhose, tricot.

**canvas** 1. Cotton, linen, or synthetic in an even heavy firm weave for sails and industrial purposes. 2. *Ada* or *Java canvas* is a stiff open-weave fabric used for yarn needlework. 3. *Awning-stripe canvas* has printed or woven stripes. 4. *Cross-stitch* or *Penelope canvas* has stiff open mesh and is used for fine cross-stitch work. 5. *Unbleached linen canvas* is used for interfacing.

**Caprolan** Trademark owned by Allied Chemical Co. for nylon filament fiber, type 6.

**Captiva** Trademark owned by Allied Chemical Co. for producer-textured nylon hosiery yarn.

**carded yarn**  Cotton yarn in which fibers are separated and aligned in a thin web, then condensed into a continuous, untwisted strand called a *sliver*. Carding removes most of the impurities of the fiber. Cheaper cottons are simply carded. More expensive ones go through an additional cleaning and combing process called *combing*.

**carpet**  A floor-covering fabric either woven, knitted, tufted, flocked, or needle punched, and made from a variety of textile fibers. Usually sold by the yard. (See broadloom.)

**carrickmacross lace**  Irish lace that has appliquéd motifs of lawn sprigs with buttonholed edges connected by knotted hexagonals like a guipure.

**cashmere**  Downy glossy undercoat hair of the cashmere goat which makes soft-yarn fine fabrics and sweaters. Often combined with wool, cotton, silk. The terms "cashmere," "Kashmir," and "Cassimere" are often used to describe a type of pattern that is also known as "paisley" and "Persian."

**cationic**  Cationic dyeable fiber is the newest tool in the fashion designer's kit. It's a dye technique that allows certain fibers (like polyester) to take deep and brilliant colors. When cationic fiber is mixed with conventional fiber various multicolors and cross-dye effects can be achieved from a single dye bath.

**Cat's Eye**  Trademark owned by Wm. Skinner & Sons (Indian Head Mills) for a fabric that is made partly of Flecton, a trademarked material that reflects light at night, invented by Minnesota Mining & Manufacturing.

**Cedilla**  Trademark owned by Fiber Industries, marketing arm of Celanese Fibers Co., for nylon 66 filament yarn for texturizing.

**Celabond**  Trademark owned by Celanese Fibers Co. for bonded fabrics backed with Celanese acetate tricot.

**Celacloud**  Trademark owned by Celanese Fibers Co. for crimped staple acetate fiber used in battings.

**Celacrimp**  Trademark owned by Celanese Fibers Co. for bulked acetate filament yarn used in tufted or chenille fabrics.

**Celafil**  Trademark owned by Celanese Fibers Co. for modified cross-section acetate yarn. Used primarily for pillows and comforters.

**Celaire**  Trademark owned by Celanese Fibers Co. for twist-set acetate and nylon filament yarns for home-furnishing markets.

**Celairese**  Trademark owned by Celanese Fibers Co. for dull staple acetate fiber.

**Celaloft**  Trademark owned by Celanese Fibers Co., for bulked acetate filament yarns, primarily for decorative fabrics.

**Celanese**  Trademark owned by Celanese Fibers Co., originally applied to cellulose acetate staple, filament, yarn, and fabric, and now broadened to include all products made by the company, such as plastics, chemicals, etc.

**Celaperm**  Trademark owned by Celanese Fibers Co. for solution-dyed acetate yarn.

**Celara**  A merchandising trademark of Celanese Fibers Co. for textiles made of textured acetate yarns.

**Celarandom**  Trademark owned by Celanese Fibers Co. for intermittently saponified acetate filament yarn.

**Celaspun**  Trademark owned by Celanese Fibers Co. for spun acetate yarn.

**3 3**

**Celatow**   Trademark owned by Celanese Fibers Co. for acetate tow yarns.

**Celatress**   Trademark owned by Celanese Fibers Co. for a special acetate filament yarn used by wig and toy industry.

**Celaweb**   Trademark owned by Celanese Fibers Co for acetate filament roving used for making cigarette filters.

**cellulose**   Organic woody substance found in vegetation which is the base of rayon and acetate fiber.

**cellulose acetate**   Filaments made of an acetic acid ester of cellulose which has been coagulated or solidified in a spinning solution after being metered through a spinneret.

**Cerex**   Trademark owned by Monsanto Co. for new spun-bonded (non-woven) nylon fabric that stretches and recovers its shape, simulating a knit fabric.

**Chadolon**   Trademark owned by Chadbourn for a nylon stretch yarn developed by Patentex.

**challis**   Various soft, supple, very lightweight, plain-weave fabrics, often printed in small floral, Persian, or cravat effects. Originated from Indian term "shallee," meaning "soft."

**chambray**   Popular cotton fabric in plain weave combining colored warp and white filling yarns. May be carded or combed. Made also in stripes, checks, and dobby designs.

**chameleon fibers**   Experimental fibers under development in Japan that are made from phototropic fiber-forming materials that change colors optically under varying light sources.

**chantilly**   Bobbin lace with fine six-sided mesh ground, pattern outlined in heavy thread. Design is usually elaborate, with scrolls and florals.

**Chavacete**  Trademark for a bulked textured-acetate yarn developed by Moulinage in France. Chavanoz of Rhodia is exclusive USA producer and supplier.

**check**  Small pattern of squares woven or printed. May be yarn dyed or cross dyed; appears in all fibers, blends, and mixtures.

**cheese**  A cylindrical package of yarn wound on a paper core or wooden tube. It somewhat resembles a wheel of cheese.

**chenille**  A fuzzy yarn whose pile resembles a caterpillar. Yarn is used mainly in decorative fabrics. Sometimes used to refer to fabric woven from chenille yarns.

**cheviot**  1. Twill similar to serge but with slightly rough napped surface. Originally made of wool from sheep of the Cheviot Hills between England and Scotland. 2. Striped or checked cotton shirting made of coarse yarns.

**cheviot tweeds**  Differ from other tweeds in that warp and filling are the same color. Wide range of colors and qualities. Usually twilled diagonally or woven in chevrons.

**chevron**  Herringbone weave or knit effect, or print in similar zigzag stripes.

**chiffon**  Very light transparent thin fabric in plain weave. The term "chiffon" is often used to indicate lightness and softness; e.g. chiffon taffeta, chiffon velvet, etc.

**chinchilla cloth**  Heavy, spongy woolen coating with napped surface rolled into little tufts or nubs by a special finishing process.

**chino**  A twilled cotton fabric of combed two-ply yarn. Usually vat dyed, mercerized, and preshrunk. Used mainly for uniforms, sportswear, hobby clothing.

**chintz** Glazed cotton fabric often printed with gay figures, birds, and florals. There are several types of glaze. Wax glaze and starched glaze, produced by use of friction or glazing calenders, wash out in laundering. A durable glaze is achieved by calendered resin finishing.

**chlorination** Process used on wool to reduce felting, thus reducing shrinkage.

**Chlorofibre** Generic term proposed by Rhovyl to replace vinyon.

**Chromeflex** Trademark owned by Metal Film Co. for non-tarnishing aluminum yarn laminated with Mylar polyester plastic.

**Chromeflex NL** Trademark owned by Metal Film Co. for non-laminated metallic yarn.

**Chromspun** Trademark owned by Eastman Chemical Products Inc. for solution-dyed acetate filament yarn, staple, and tow.

**circular knit** See jersey.

**ciré** Lustrous patent-leather effect produced on the surface of a fabric.

**ciselé** Velvet with a pattern formed by contrast in cut and uncut loops.

**Civona** Trademark owned by Du Pont for hollow-filament rayon yarn.

**clan plaid** Scottish plaid in colors identifying a Scottish clan. The clans are: Brodie; Bruce; Buchanan; Cameron; Cameron (Erracht); Cameron (Lochiel); Campbell (Argyll); Campbell (Breadalbane); Campbell (Cawdor); Campbell (Loudon); Chisholm; Colquhoun; Cumin or Cumming; Davidson; Douglas; Drummond; Duff and MacDuff; Erskine; Farquharson; Ferguson; Forbes; Forty-Second Royal Highland Regiment (Black Watch); Fraser; Gordon; Gow and MacGowan; Graham; Grant; Gunn; Hay; Henderson; Innes; Johnston; Kennedy; Lamont; Leslie; Lindsay; Loga or MacLennan; MacAlister; Mac-Alpine; MacArthur; MacAulay; MacCallum or Malcolm; MacDonald; MacDonald (Clanranald); MacDonald (Sleate); MacDonell (Glengarry); MacDonell (Keppoch); MacDougall; MacEwen; MacFarlane; Macfie or MacPhee; MacGillivray; MacGregor; MacInnes (Aonghais); MacIntyre; MacKay; Mac-Kenzie; MacKinlay; MacKinnon; Mackintosh; MacLachlan; MacLaren; Maclaine (Lochbuie); Maclean; Macleod (Macleod); Macleod (Lewis); MacMillan; MacNab; MacNaughton; Mac-Neil (Barra); McNeill (Colonsay); Macpherson; Macpherson (Hunting); Macquarrie; Macqueen; Macrae; Matheson; Men-zies; Morrison; Munro; Murray (Atholl); Murray (Tullibardine); Ogilvie; Robertson or Donnachaidh; Rose; Ross; Scott; Sinclair; Skene; Stewart (Appin); Stewart (Atholl); Stewart (Dress); Stewart (Hunting); Stewart (Royal); Sutherland; Urquhart.

**classic** Term often used in fashion to describe traditional style, pattern, design, etc.

**clip-dot or -spot fabrics** Figured fabrics decorated with small contrasting woven spots of extra warp or filling yarn. Floating threads between the spots are clipped or sheared in finishing. Either side may be used as the face.

**cloque** French word for blister-effect matelassé weave. Some-times anglicized into "cloky."

**Cluny** Medium-weight to heavyweight bobbin lace with "wheat-ear" or "wheel" designs.

**Clupak** Trademark owned by Clupak, Inc., for non-woven stretchable paper fabric invented by Sanford Cluett.

**coachman's cloth** See beaver cloth; kersey; melton.

**coated fabrics**  Fabrics coated, covered, or treated with various substances to make them waterproof, flameproof, etc. Coating substances include rubber, resins, plastics, melamines, oil finishes, etc.

**Coin**  Trademark owned by Coin International, division of Coin Sales Corp., for a bonded process that joins two fabrics together permanently by use of certain adhesives. The firm licenses its process to fabric that meets certain tests and quality standards. Other Coin marks: *Coin-Puff; Coin-Vertible; Coin-Flex; 2-Faced.*

**Coloray**  Trademark owned by Courtaulds N.A. for solution-dyed viscose rayon staple fiber.

**colorfast**  Term used to describe fabrics that keep their shades without fading during the normal life of a garment. Strictly speaking, no fabric is absolutely "colorfast." Dyestuffs used in apparel and home furnishings have colorfast ratings in terms of hours.

**Color-Sealed**  Trademark owned by Du Pont for solution-dyed filament and staple yarns of all types of fibers.

**Colorspun**  Trademark owned by American Viscose Division of FMC Corp. for solution-dyed acetate and rayon yarns. Now renamed *Avicolor.*

**combed cotton**  Cotton yarn that is cleaned after carding by wire brushes (combs) and roller cards to remove all short fibers and impurities. More expensive than carded cottons.

**Comiso**  Trademark owned by Beaunit Fibers for high-tenacity rayon staple fiber and tow.

**Coneprest**  Trademark owned by Cone Mills for its durable-press process.

**conjugate fiber**  See bicomponent fiber.

**continuous filament**  A long continuous strand of a manufactured fiber as distinguished from all natural fibers (except raw silk), which are of short staple or length.

**Contro**  Trademark owned by Firestone for rubber elastic yarn.

**converter**  Distributor of fabrics who buys gray goods, styles them, has them finished to his order to sell to cutters and retail stores. Many mills that weave gray goods have their own converting departments. The converters' trade association is called Textile Distributors Association.

**copolymer**  A fiber spun from two variants of same liquor. A *homopolymer* has only one.

**Cordura**  Trademark owned by Du Pont for bulked-filament nylon yarn; used in woven fabrics for industrial uses, shoe uppers, luggage; also used for twine.

**corduroy**  Cut-pile fabric woven with either wide or narrow wales formed by using extra filling. Back may be either plain or twill weave, the latter being better quality.

**core spinning**  Yarn process for sheathing fine-denier elastomeric spandex yarns under tension with non-stretch fibers. There are many patented techniques for core spinning, all designed to create fabrics with stretch characteristics and performance. The internal member is called the *core yarn*.

**core twist**  Newest trick in creating stretch yarns is to sheath a fine-denier elastomeric spandex core with a textured stretch yarn. Fabrics made of these yarns have beefed-up stretch and recovery properties.

**Coronizing**  Trademark owned by Owens-Corning Fiberglas Corp. for a special finish for glass textiles that provides a soft mellow hand, good drapability, and crease resistance. It is a resin treatment applied under very high heat.

**Corval** Trademark owned by Courtaulds (N.A.) Inc. for cross-linked rayon fiber to blend with wool and synthetics.

**Cotron** Trademark owned by American Viscose Division of FMC Corp. for fabric containing 70% cotton and 30% Avisco rayon (plus or minus 5%), which meets certain standards.

**cotton** Soft vegetable fiber obtained from seed pod of the cotton plant. First known in India about 3,000 B.C. The longer the fiber, the better the quality. Lengths vary from less than one-half inch to over two inches; usually they are about one inch. Most cotton is creamy white, but it may be tawny, brownish, reddish, etc. Annual production in the United States is in excess of ten million bales. A bale of cotton usually weighs 500 pounds.

**count** In textiles, three meanings: 1. Number size of a yarn. 2. Number of ends and picks per inch of weave, or their sum, as 80x80 percale, or 200-count sheeting. 3. Number of wales and courses per inch in a knitted fabric.

**course** A row of stitches across a knitted fabric. Corresponds to the weft (or filling) in woven goods.

**covert** Medium-to-heavy weave in a finely flecked diagonal twill made of tightly twisted two-ply yarns, one woolen, the other contrasting white wool, cotton, rayon, or silk. *Venetian covert,* usually a coating weight, has a highly lustrous finish.

**crash** Coarse toweling weave made of thick uneven yarns. In various weights.

**cravat** Covering and decoration for the neck prior to the introduction of neckties. Also another name for a four-in-hand necktie. Small prints and weaves typical of necktie cloths are often called "cravat patterns."

**Cravenette** Trademark owned by the Cravenette Corp. for a water-repellent process. Named for Craven, its inventor.

**crease resistant**  Term used to describe fabrics that have been treated or constructed to make them resistant to wrinkling. One of the most common methods is to incorporate a certain amount of synthetic resin. (See durable press.)

**crepes**  Fabrics with pebbly, crinkled, or puckered surfaces obtained by engineering these characteristics into the yarn or by calendering fabrics in the finishing process. There are sheer crepes, such as georgettes, and heavy sheer crepes. Flat crepes and crepes de chine are medium weights. Canton crepes, marocain crepes, satin crepes, and satin-backed crepes are heavier types.

**crepe-back satins**  Sometimes called *satin-back crepes;* are finished on both sides to be reversible. Some may be finished on satin or dull face only.

**crepe de chine**  Fine plain crepe in light to medium and even heavy suit weights, made of twisted silk in both directions of the weave. Originated in China.

**Crepeset**  A trademark owned by American Enka Corp. for a patented process of yarn modification applied to nylon while in the unfinished or partially processed state. The crepe yarns obtained via such a process are referred to as "producer textured" to distinguish them from those textured yarn effects produced by throwsters.

**crepon**  Heavy crepe with lengthwise crinkles. Sometimes patterned with large jacquard designs.

**Creslan**  Trademark owned by American Cyanamid Co. for acrylic staple and filament fibers.

**cretonne**  A drapery or slipcover fabric named after the Frenchman who first made it. Usually printed, similar to unglazed chintz, and made of an Osnaburg-base fabric.

**crimp**   Waviness in fibers, natural or manufactured.

**crinoline**   1. Open stiff weave with hard-twist cotton warp and horsehair filling. 2. Fabric with a firm starched or permanent resin finish (cheesecloth, sheeting, etc.) 3. Stiff, bouffant petticoat.

**crochet**   A fabric, article, trimming, or lace made by interlocking loops or stitches with a hook in plain or fancy pattern.

**crocking**   Rubbing off of color as a result of improper dye, poor penetration, or fixation.

**cross-dyed effects**   Multicolored effects produced in one dye bath from fabrics containing fibers with different affinities to the same dye. (See cationic.)

**cross-linking**   A chemical process for modifying the molecular structure of a fiber by forming a permanent bond or link. Usually improves crease resistance or dyeability.

**Crystal**   A trademark owned by Tennessee Eastman (marketed by Eastman Chemical Fibers) for a plain cross-section filament acetate fiber.

**Cumuloft**   Trademark owned by Monsanto Fibers for texturized nylon filament carpet yarn.

**Cupioni**   Trademark owned by Beaunit Fibers for thick-and-thin cuprammonium rayon filament patterned after silk doupion.

**Cupracolor**   Trademark owned by Beaunit Fibers for solution-dyed cuprammonium rayon filament.

**cuprammonium**   Classified as rayon but differs from viscose rayon fiber in chemical composition and in being "stretch spun" in its coagulating bath during the process of manufacture. Bemberg is only firm making it in the U.S.

**Cuprasil**  Trademark owned by Beaunit Fibers for a special textured cuprammonium rayon yarn.

**Cuprel**  Trademark owned by Beaunit Fibers for slubbed rayon textured yarn that has been air bulked.

**Cuprino**  A trademark owned by Beaunit Fibers for a textured filament and slubbed rayon yarn.

**Cuprofino**  Textured filling yarn of cuprammonium rayon and polyester combining filament or spun fibers in a single yarn.

**Cyana**  Trademark owned by American Cyanamid Co. and used as a prefix for a number of textile finishes.

**cyanoethylation**  Treatment of cotton fibers with acrylonitrile and caustic soda to alter their nature—makes them stronger, easier to dye, and less susceptible to rot.

**Cycloset**  Designation used by Du Pont for acetate yarns engineered for good mill performance without the need for twisting.


# D

**D-225**  Trademark owned by Owens-Corning for fine-denier glass filament yarns. Used mainly for curtains and draperies.

**Dacron**  Trademark owned by Du Pont for polyester filaments and staple fibers.

**damask**  Firm, patterned, glossy jacquard weave, flatter than brocade; brought to Damascus by Marco Polo in the 13th century.

**Dan-Press**   Trademark owned by Dan River Mills for its polyester-cotton durable-press process.

**Darvan**   Trademark for a nytril (FTC generic term) fiber by Celanese Corporation of America. Not now being produced in the U.S. Called *Travis* in West Germany. Licensed for production in Japan.

**Dawbac**   Trademark owned by Dawbarn for olefin carpet backing.

**Day-Glo**   Trademark for a daylight fluorescent color imparting extreme brilliance under daylight or night conditions, patented by Switzer Bros., Inc.

**decating**   Finishing process for fabric which forces steam through layers of a roll of cloth. The steam is withdrawn rapidly with a vacuum pump and the roll cooled. The fibers and yarns swell and rearrange themselves so as to produce a smooth finish, free of wrinkles, with a lofty hand.

**decorticating**   Process of removing woody residual matter from bast fibers, like flax, after retting.

**deep-pile fabrics**   Wide range of fabrics woven or knitted to simulate various furs or pelts, such as astrakhan, chinchilla, beaver, ermine, mink, leopard, etc. FTC forbids use of fur names; labels and advertising must indicate that material is a cloth.

**degumming**   Process of boiling silk in a hot soapy bath to remove the natural gum.

**delustering**   Dulling or eliminating luster of yarns or fabric by using titanium (pigment) in the fiber solution, or various chemicals during yarn or cloth finishing.

**4 4**

**Delustra** Trademark owned by Courtaulds for a dull rayon filament yarn produced in England.

**denier** Unit of weight indicating size of a fiber filament based on weight in grams of a standard strand of 9,000 meters. The higher the denier number the heavier the yarn. Used in connection with silk, rayon, acetate, and most man-made fibers.

**denim** Washable, inexpensive, strong, twilled cotton cloth made of single yarn. Usually made with colored warp and white filling but may also be piece dyed or woven in fancy plaids, dobbies, stripes, and two-color iridescent effects. Sometimes printed, scuffed, scrubbed, brushed, faded to achieve new fashion looks.

**Diamond** Trademark owned by Metlon Corp. for a clear plastic flat yarn.

**Diamond Black** Trademark owned by Beaunit Fibers for solution-dyed cupra rayon filament yarn.

**Diane** Trademark owned by Sauquoit Fibers Co. for a false-twist stretch yarn.

**diaper cloth** Usually a soft absorbent cotton fabric bleached white. Four main types are: (1) birdseye dobby weave, (2) soft plain cotton flannel, (3) twill weave, (4) plain knit.

**Diaphan** Trademark owned by Heberlein for woven or knit fabrics made of Helanca textured yarns.

**dimity** Sheer fabric with lengthwise cords or checks formed by bunching two, three, or more warp and filling threads together. Usually made of combed cotton.

**direct dyes** Class of dyestuffs that colors cellulosic fibers in full shades without the use of fixatives. Also known as *substantive dyes*.

**direct print**   Pattern and ground color printed on fabric in the colors desired, as opposed to extract printing done on a dyed cloth. Cretonne is an example of a direct print.

**discharge or extract print**   Designs printed by removal of some of the color from a previously dyed fabric. A design in a different color may be imprinted simultaneously. Cheaper than application or direct printing.

**DLP**   Trademark owned by Dawbarn Manufacturing Co. for polyolefin multifilament and olefin monofilament yarns.

**dobby**   Fabric with geometric figures woven in a set pattern. Similar to, but more limited, more quickly woven, and cheaper than jacquards, which require elaborate procedures to form patterns.

**doeskin finish**   Nap finish on woolens that covers the weave completely. After fabrics have been fulled, fibers are drawn to the surface, straightened, and combed in one direction. Used on flannel, billiard cloth, etc.

**Donegal**   Thick homespun woolen tweed handwoven in Ireland, named for country where it is made. Name protected by a county association. Characteristics are thick spots or slubs of several different colors woven irregularly into the fabric.

**dope dyed**   Trade slang for "solution dyed" or "spun dyed," meaning that color is put into the chemical liquid from which rayon, acetate, or synthetic fibers are drawn. Filaments emerge colored.

**Dorzan**   Trademark owned by Du Pont for woven material of Du Pont fibers for footwear and accessories.

**dotted swiss**   Various cottons, mostly sheers, ornamented with small dots. Originally the dots were produced by swivel weaving, but now other methods are used, including clipped spots, flock print imitations, etc. Dots may be the same or different

**4 6**

color. The original is still made in Switzerland and imported into the U.S.

**double-cloth** Two separate cloths combined in weaving through use of binding threads. Face and back may contrast in weave and color.

**double-face satin** Satin cloth made with two warps and one filling to obtain satin effects on both face and neck.

**double knit** Firm, often reversible knitted fabric made on a special knitting machine that combines a double set of needles to produce one fabric.

**doupion** Silk thread made from two cocoons united by two worms spinning close together. Yarn is uneven, irregular, and thicker than that from one cocoon. Used in slubbed fabrics such as shantung. Doupion is French name. Also called *douppioni* (Italian) and *dupion* (English).

**Drapespun** Trademark owned by American Cyanamid for rayon filament yarn used in draperies.

**drawing** 1. The hot or cold stretching of fibers to increase orientation and reduce size. 2. Process of repeated drafting of fiber slivers on a carding machine and doubling and redoubling of the slivers.

**Dream Slub** Trademark owned by Beaunit Fibers for rayon novelty yarns with torpedo-shaped slubs.

**drill** Strong twilled carded cotton cloth. Used for work clothing, uniforms, etc.

**drip-dry** Market phrase coined to describe clothes and fabrics which after washing are hung on a hanger to drip and dry without wringing. With the great growth recorded in installation of home dryers in wired houses less and less goods are being drip-dried. (See durable press.)

**Dual Torque**   Trademark owned by Fluflon for a high-torque yarn with alternating twist.

**duchesse satin**   Satin weave with plain back and crisp texture, lustrous and smooth.

**duck**   Commonly used for canvas. Name comes from Dutch word "doek," meaning cloth.

**Ducle**   Trademark owned by Meyers for a false-twist high-bulked nylon yarn.

**Duloft**   Trademark owned by Duplan for a stretch, bulked, or torque yarn of nylon or polyester.

**Duotwist**   Trademark owned by Turbo for a false-twist yarn-texturizing machine.

**duplex prints**   Designs printed on both face and back of fabrics in two distinct operations, usually to get woven effect.

**durable press**   Important technological development in textiles that achieves the ultimate in wash-and-wear—requires absolutely no ironing during the normal use-life of a garment. The term applies to apparel and other textile products such as sheets, draperies, etc. (Often called *permanent press*.) Durable press is hailed as one of the most significant and far-reaching developments in the history of textiles—one that rivals in importance the development of man-made fibers. As a rule, DP is achieved in two ways: 1. Pre-curing fabrics with a special resin finish; then pressing made-up garment with a hot-head press to impart the no-iron feature. 2. Post-curing fabric with a resin finish; then cooking made-up garments in an oven to bake in or set the wash-and-wear features. As a rule, polyester-cotton blends are most popular, but there are 100% cottons and other blends that work well. Launched in men's slacks to keep crease in and wrinkles out by Koret of California—with their patented Koratron process—the DP concept has spread like wildfire through the entire textile industry. Zippers, findings, linings all are being made to fit in with DP concepts; and traditional manufacturing and sewing techniques are being changed and modified. Under evaluation now, but still some time away, are other curing methods including use of gamma rays, dipping, ultra-high-frequency waves, etc. Newest approach via fiber blends of polyester and cellulosics require no resin. (See Koratron, post-curing, pre-curing.)

**Duramil** Trademark owned by Deering Milliken & Co. Inc. for a durable, water-repellent, spot- and crease-resistant finish.

**Duraspan** Trademark owned by International Playtex for its monofilament elastomeric spandex yarns. (See Stretch-Ever.)

**Durastran** Trademark owned by Multi-tex for a metallic polyester-laminated aluminum-foil yarn.

**Durel** Trademark owned by Celanese Fibers Co. for a slit-film olefin carpet yarn. Limited production.

**Durene** Trademark for mercerized cotton yarns, knit goods, and fabrics, owned by Durene Association of America.

**Durenka** Trademark owned by American Enka Corp. for high-strength viscose rayon staple.

**Dutex** Trademark owned by Duplan Corp. for stretched, bulked, or crimped nylon or polyester yarns.

**duvetyn** Twill with a napped velvety surface that hides the weave. Originally made by Rodier. Cotton duvetyn, also called *cotton suede*, is converted from soft filled heavy sheeting, napped, sheared, and felted.

**Dye 1** Trademark owned by Monsanto Fibers for a cationic dyeable modified nylon 66 filament yarn.

**dyeing**  Process of applying color to fiber, yarn, or fabric. Major methods are: *bale dyeing* (low-cost method for cotton) . . . *batik dyeing* (see batik) . . . *beam dyeing* (warp is dyed prior to weaving) . . . *Burl* or *speck dyeing* (hand operation for woolens to cover specks or burls in fabric . . . *chain dyeing* (continuous process, fabrics tacked end to end) . . . *cross dyeing* (two or more colors obtained in one dye bath) . . . *jig dyeing* (cloth processed in jig, vat, kier, or vessel) . . . *package dyeing* (yarns dyed while on cones, cakes, or cheeses) . . . *piece dyeing* (dyeing of fabric in cut, bolt, or piece form) . . . *random dyeing* (coloring only certain areas of a fabric or yarn) . . . *raw-stock dyeing* (dyeing of raw fiber prior to spinning into yarn) . . . *resist dyeing* (treating fabric surfaces so that treated portions will resist a subsequent dye operation by repelling dyestuff) . . . *solution dyeing* (pigment or color is fixed into a fiber during the spinning process; sometimes fabric is called "dope dyed" or "spun dyed") . . . *stock dyed* (fibers dyed after degreasing and drying; usually refers to woolen or worsted stock prior to blending, carding, and spinning into yarn) . . . *top dyed* (dyeing or printing of worsted top or sliver in loose formation) . . . *union dyed* (coloring of two or more different textile fibers in one dyebath) . . . *vat dyed* (dyeing by use of vat dyes—an extremely fast dyestuff; originally done in huge wooden vats on cellulosic fabric only, hence the name) . . . *yarn dyeing* (yarn dyed prior to weaving into cloth).

**dyes**  Natural or synthetic colorings for textiles. Dyes differ in resistance to sunlight, perspiration, washing, gas, alkali, etc.; effectiveness on different fibers; reaction to cleaning agents; solubility; and methods of application.

**Dylanize**  Trademark owned by Stevensons (Dyers) Ltd. (UK) for a process to control shrinkage of woolens.

**Dy-Cor**  Trademark owned by Hess Goldsmith for a dyeing technique to achieve tone-on-tone or cross-dye effects on glass fabrics by piece dyeing.

**Dy-Lok**  Trademark owned by American Cyanamid for solution-dyed rayon filament yarns.

**Dynabelt**   Trademark owned by FMC for high-modulus rayon tire cord.

**Dynaloft**   Trademark owned by Leon-Ferenbach for textured nylon or polyester yarn.

**Dynel**   Trademark owned by Union Carbide Corp. for mod-acrylic staple fiber.


## E

**"E"**   Trademark owned by Owens-Corning for glass fiber.

**Easthampton**   Trademark owned by United Elastic Corp. for monofilament spandex fiber and yarns.

**Eastman**   Trademark owned by Tennessee Eastman for acetate fibers marketed by Eastman Chemical Products Inc. (See Estron).

**écossais**   Satin-striped fabric using two colors—one color in lengthwise satin stripes standing out on the face, the other in the underlying plain weave, which may be barred or checked.

**ècru**   Beige color of raw or unbleached fabrics, linens, silks, and laces.

**EF 121**   (See Source.)

**Egyptian cotton**   Egypt is the world's largest producer of high-grade, long-staple cotton, grown mostly in the Nile Delta. Commonly runs from 1 1/8 to 1 1/2 inches long. The fibers are quite fine and vary in color from light cream to dark tan.

**Ektafill**   Trademark owned by Eastman Chemical for polyester fiberfill for furniture batting.

**elastomer**   Elastic fiber such as synthetic rubber or spandex having the physical stretch properties of natural rubber.

**Elder**   Trademark owned by Toray of Japan for fusible sewing thread for joining fabrics by pressing with hot iron.

**elongation**   Deformation of a fiber due to stretching. Measured as a percentage of the original length.

**Elura**   Trademark of Monsanto for new modacrylic filament fiber designed specifically for wigs.

**embossed**   Figures or designs raised on the surface of fabrics, usually with engraved, heated rollers.

**embroidery**   Ornamental needlework done on fabric with threads, by machine or hand.

**Encron**   Trademark owned by American Enka Corp. for round cross-section polyester staple and filament and high-tenacity feeder yarns for texturizing.

**Encron Plus**   Merchandising trademark of American Enka Corp. designating fabric blends of Encron polyester and Zantrel or Zantrel 700 high-modulus rayon.

**end**   One thread of the warp; also a remnant of fabric.

**end-and-end**   Weave with two colors alternating in warp yarns.

**Enkaloft**   Trademark owned by American Enka Corp. for high-bulk textured filament nylon carpet yarn.

**Enkalure**   Trademark owned by American Enka Corp. for multilobal nylon filament yarns, producer textured, with sparkle, glitter, and silk-like hand.

**Enka Nylon**   Trademark owned by American Enka Corp. for nylon fiber.

**Enka Polyester**  Trademark owned by American Enka Corp. for regular and high-tenacity filament polyester and feeder yarns.

**Enka Rayon**  Trademarks owned by American Enka Corp. for rayon fibers of various lusters designated with trademark names: *Briglo* (bright), *Perglo* (semi-dull), *Englo* (dull).

**Enkasheer**  Trademark owned by American Enka Corp. for producer-modified nylon yarns for stretch-hosiery fields.

**Enkatron**  Trademark owned by American Enka Corp. for un-textured trilobal cross-section filament nylon carpet yarns.

**Enkor**  Trademark owned by American Enka Corp. for high-modulus viscose rayon staple.

**Enkrome**  Merchandising trademark owned by American Enka Corp. for promotion of fabrics containing acid-dyeable rayon filament and staple fibers.

**entredeux**  French for a very narrow hemstitch machine-embroidered insertion used in seams of lingerie, blouses, and baby clothes.

**épinglé**  French for fine, lustrous, corded dress goods or ribbons with large and small ribs alternating in the same or different color.

**éponge**  Soft, spongy weave made of yarn with uneven, nubby twist. Name derives from French word for "sponge."

**Escon**  Trademark owned by Enjay Fibers for monofilament olefin fiber.

**Estane V.C.**  Trademark owned by Goodrich for spandex elastomeric yarn.

**Estron**   Trademark owned by Eastman Chemical Products, Inc. for acetate filament yarns, staple, fiber, and tow.

**etamine**   Lightweight open plain weave made in many different weights and many different fibers or blends.

**Eural**   Merchandising trademark owned by Rhodiaceta for approved end products made of Tergal polyester in France.

**Eurat**   Merchandising trademark owned by Rhodiaceta for approved end products made of Tergal polyester in West Germany.

**Everglaze**   Trademark signifying fabric processed and tested according to standards controlled by Joseph Bancroft & Sons Co.

**extract prints**   See discharge prints.

**eyelash**   Fabric spotted with fringed oblongs that look like eyelashes.

## F

**Faboucle**   Trademark owned by Madison Throwing Co. for stretch and textured filament yarns of all types.

**fabric**   Any woven, knitted, plaited, braided, felted, or non-woven material made of fibers or yarns may be termed a fabric. In the broad sense fabric may be defined as any stuff made on a loom or a knitting or needling machine . . . usually described as apparel, decorative, or industrial types.

**Fabutex**   Trademark owned by Madison Throwing Co. for stretch and textured filament yarns of all types.

**faconné**  French term for a figured fabric.

**faille**  Fabric with flat horizontal ribs. Common in crepes, such as tissue faille and canton faille.

**Fairtex**  Trademark owned by Fairtex Corp. for metallic fiber of aluminum foil and butyrate (acetate) or Mylar (polyester) film.

**fall-on prints**  Designs in which colors are applied over each other to get several different colors.

**false twist**  Most widely used yarn-texturizing process. Thermoplastic yarn is twisted . . . heat set . . . then untwisted. The memory of the yarn causes it to bulk and stretch. (See heat set.)

**fancies**  Fabrics with patterned weaves; any fabric that is not plain.

**feather cloth**  Fabric in which feather fluff is introduced for softness or decoration.

**featherstitch**  Decorative blanket stitches branching from a main vein, as from the shaft of a feather.

**feeder yarn**  Yarn supplied by a fiber producer to a throwster ready for texturizing.

**felt**  Compact sheet of matted fibers of wool, fur, or mohair, often mixed with cotton or rayon. The raw material is thoroughly mixed, carded, and hardened with the aid of moisture, heat, and pressure. Finest felts are fur and mohair. Very light weights are supported with a sheer nylon core.

**fiber**  Any tough substance, natural or man made, composed of thread-like tissue capable of being spun, woven, or knitted.

55

**Fiber 25**  Acetate filament yarn with bulky qualities produced by FMC. Other FMC yarns include *Fiber 40* and *Fiber 43* high-tenacity rayons with high wet modulus.

**Fiber 52**  A nylon filament yarn produced by Fiber Industries.

**Fiber 200**  Staple and filament polyester yarn produced by FMC.

**Fiber 410**  High-wet-strength rayon yarn with low shrink properties made by FMC.

**Fiber 700**  High-wet-modulus rayon staple yarn produced by American Enka Corp.

**Fiber "B"**  Trademark owned by Beaunit Fibers for high-tenacity, high-wet-modulus rayon staple fiber.

**Fiber "HM"**  High-wet-modulus polynosic fiber that may be identified by trademark *Zantrel,* owned by American Enka Corp.

**Fiber "RD" 101**  Specialty fiber made by FMC as a short self-bonding rayon staple for use in paper and wet-formed non-woven materials.

**Fiber "Y"**  See Qiana.

**Fiberbond**  Trademark owned by Union Carbide for non-woven material used as batting or cushioning for furniture or autos.

**Fibercoil**  Trademark owned by Du Pont for polyester spray-bonded batting or filling material for furniture.

**fiberfill**  Generic name for stuffing fibers used in battings, quiltings, pillows, etc.

**Fiberfrax**  Trademark owned by Carborundum for alumina-silica high-temperature specialty fibers used mainly in electrical insulation.

**Fiberglas**  Trademark owned by Owens-Corning Fiberglas Corp. for fine-filament glass fiber.

**Fiberset**  Trademark owned by Bianchini, Ferier, Inc., for a process that stabilizes rayon fabrics.

**fibranne**  Generic French term for viscose rayon staple.

**Fibravyl**  See Rhovy.

**fibrene**  Generic French term for spun rayon yarns.

**Fibrid**  Trademark owned by Du Pont for a unique fibrous form of synthetic polymeric materials—acrylic, nylon, polyester —that serves as binder for non-woven fabrics called textryls produced on paper-making equipment. (See spunbonded.)

**fibrillation**  Term used to describe split-film fibers or yarns. Yarn is extruded as ribbon or tape rather than fine filament; then tape is split.

**Fibro**  Trademark owned by Courtaulds North America Inc. for rayon staple fiber.

**Fila-Crimp**  Trademark owned by Textured Yarn Co. for textured yarn of nylon or polyester.

**filament**  Single continuous strand of silk, rayon, acetate, and synthetic fibers. Filaments are plied together and spun into yarn.

**Filatex**  Trademark owned by Filatex Corp. for covered rubber elastic yarn or extruded rubber thread.

**filature**   Factory in which raw silk is reeled from cocoons.

**filet lace**   Lace with knotted square-mesh ground and square design in darned or woven effect.

**filling**   Crosswise yarn in a weave. Synonyms are *weft* and *woof*. Filling is also a term for sizing substances, such as china clay or starch, used to give body or weight to a cloth.

**finish**   General term for processes used in converting gray goods into finished cloth. Bleaching, mercerizing, steaming, singeing, dyeing are typical finishing processes.

**Firestone**   Trademark owned by Firestone Synthetic Fibers Co. for nylon yarns.

**Flaikona**   Trademark owned by Beaunit Fibers for continuous filament rayon flake yarn.

**flake**   Novelty fabric made of ply yarns in which soft, unusually colored flakes or tufts appear at intervals, regular or random.

**Flake-Slub**   Trademark owned by Beaunit Fibers for novelty rayon yarn with short entangled slub.

**flame repellent**   Treatment, usually chemical, that makes fabrics less susceptible to flash or sustained burning.

**flannel**   Plain or twill weave with a slightly napped surface. May be yarn dyed, piece dyed, cross dyed, or have streaked stock-dyed effects.

**flannelette**   Plain cotton weave finished with a nap on one side. Also known as *kimono flannel*.

**flat crepe**   Crepe with flat yarn warp and twisted yarn filling. Flatter than crepe de chine.

**flax** Slender erect annual plant of the genus *Linum,* whose fiber, removed from the stem and processed, is used in the manufacture of linen. (See retting.)

**Flecto-flash** Trademark owned by Munsingwear, Inc., for knitwear made partly from Flecton fiber, which reflects light at night.

**Flecton** Trademark owned by Minnesota Mining & Manufacturing Co. for a mineral fiber that has the property of reflecting light at night.

**fleece** Coat of wool shorn from the living sheep, usually taken off the animal in one piece. Loosely, the term also means pile or napped fabric with a deep, soft fleecy surface.

**Flexcel** Trademark owned by Pen Silson Co. for stretch yarn twisted in combination with cotton, rayon, and other yarns.

**Flexcrepe** Trademark owned by Kahn & Feldman for stretch yarns of various types.

**float** Portion of warp or filling yarn that covers two or more adjacent filling or warp threads to form a design or a satin surface.

**flocks** Short fibrous particles of fibers or short hairs applied by various processes to the surface of a fabric. One method is to print the design in adhesive, then dust with the flocks, which adhere to the prepared portions. Usually an electrostatic charge is used to keep flocks standing vertical. This is called *electrostatic flocking.*

**Fluffbon** Trademark owned by Madison Throwing Co. for textured filament nylon yarns made via the Fluflon process.

**Fluflon** Trademark owned by Leesona Corp. for a high-stretch and high-bulk process applicable to any thermoplastic fiber.

**fluorescent fabrics**   Fabrics that glow brilliantly in either sunlight or artificial light because of special dyes or materials.

**FLW**   Trademark used by Du Pont for fluorescent white filament acetate yarn . . . also called *Acele*. (See Acele.)

**fly**   Waste fibers or particles which fly out into the air during carding, drawing, spinning, or other fiber processing.

**foam-back**   Fabric with very thin slice of synthetic foam (usually polyurethane) bonded to its underside by heat, pressure, or special adhesives.

**Formelle**   Trademark owned by Rohm and Haas for color-spun nylon hosiery yarn that retains stretch and recovery properties in pantyhose.

**Fortisan**   Trademark owned by Celanese Fibers Co. for high-tenacity rayon fiber.

**Fortrel**   Trademark owned by Fiber Industries, Inc., for polyester filament and staple.

**foulard**   Lightweight twill, often printed in cravat patterns.

**french crepe**   Very lightweight crepe for lingerie and linings.

**frieze**   Thick, heavyweight coating and upholstery fabric, with a rough raised fibrous surface and more or less hard feel.

**fringe**   Trimming of short lengths of thread, loose or twisted, variously arranged and combined. Also raveled fabric edge, twisted, plaited, or tasseled.

**frisé**   French for "curled." Applied to various weaves made of looped, knotted, or curled yarns.

**Frontera**  Trademark owned by Tennaco Chemicals for new chemical technology for creating a wide variety of textured surfaces, called sculptured polymers. Makes possible new types of fabrics and materials for apparel and home use.

**fuji**  Originally a plain spun-silk weave made in Fuji, Japan.

**fulling**  Finishing operation used on woolens which mats or felts them by pressure.

**Fybrite**  Merchandising trademark of Fiber Industries for fabrics of Fortrel polyester that pass company standards for anti-soil and anti-static properties.

**Fyrel**  Trademark owned by Fabric Research for fabrics woven from metallic filaments designed for special high-strength, high-temperature applications.

# G

**G-150**  Trademark owned by Owens-Corning for glass filament yarn used mainly for industrial or electrical fabrics or tape.

**gabardine**  Firmly woven, clear-finished, warp-faced, fine, close-set diagonal fabric with twill surface and flat back. Usually piece dyed and finished with high sheen. Also yarn dyed and cross dyed.

**galatea**  Strong warp-effect twill cotton fabric used for children's playclothes. Named for legendary Greek maiden.

**galloon**  Narrow trimming braid, embroidery, or lace. Metallic threads are sometimes interlaced, or all metallic.

**garnetting**  The shredding of yarns or waste fibers to return them to fibrous condition.

**gauffré**  French term for various embossed patterns pressed into fabrics.

**gauge**  In knit goods and hosiery, gauge signifies the number of needles per inch of width. The greater the number, the closer and usually the finer the knit.

**gauze**  Sheer open weave, similar to cheesecloth.

**georgette**  Heavy sheer crepe made of yarn twisted both ways in the weave. Usually same yarn in warp and filling.

**Gerfil**  Trademark formerly owned by Gerfil Co. for fine-denier polypropylene olefin fiber and yarn. Now owned by Phillips, but production discontinued.

**gimp**  1. Ornamental cord made of various materials, often with a wire, and sometimes with a coarse cord, running through it. 2. Cord used to outline the design in lace.

**gin**  Used loosely, it refers to cotton gin invented by Eli Whitney in 1791. It removes seeds from cotton boll mechanically.

**gingham**  Yarn-dyed bombed or carded cotton fabric woven in checks, stripes, and plaids of two or more colors.

**Glacé**  Trademark owned by Monsanto for filament acrylic fiber. (See Acrilan.) Not currently in production.

**glass**  Federal Trade Commission's generic term for glass fiber.

**glazed**  Cotton fabrics such as chintz or tarlatan treated with starch, glue, paraffin, or shellac and run through a hot friction roller to give a high polish. These types are not durable in washing. Newer, more durable methods use synthetic resins that withstand laundering.

**Glen-Bulk**   Trademark owned by Glen Raven for textured yarns of various types, including Orlon acrylic. Other names owned by firm are *Glen-Set* and *Glen Spun,* also used to define textured spun yarns.

**glen checks**   Wide variety of many-line checks originating in Scottish districts. (See Scottish district checks.)

**Glitter**   Trademark owned by Beaunit Fibers for spatter-, sparkle-effect cuprammonium rayon filament yarn with mica.

**Globe**   Trademark owned by Globe Manufacturing Co. for extruded uncovered rubber thread.

**Glospan**   Trademark owned by Globe Manufacturing Co. for a fused multifilament spandex fiber.

**Glowette**   Trademark owned by Rich-Flex for metallic yarn with textured or bulky appearance.

**gossamer**   Filmy gauze used as veiling and for drifting bouffant evening skirts.

**graft copolymerization**   A process patented by Scott Paper Co. and now under evaluation for altering fabric properties by altering fiber molecules. Will eventually be licensed when perfected.

**granite cloth**   Fabric with pebbled effects that suggests the grainy surface of unpolished granite.

**grease wool**   Raw wool shorn from the sheep. Called grease wool because it still contains natural oils . . . as much as 80% of original weight. This oil is excellent source of lanolin.

**greige**   French for fabrics in unbleached, undyed state before finishing. In U.S., *gray goods* or *grey goods.* Greige also describes a color between gray and beige.

**grenadine**   Fine, loosely woven fabric in leno weave similar to marquisette, with clipped dobby design. Also tie fabric in open construction.

**Grip**   A merchandising trademark of Monsanto Fibers for polyester clothing under the firm's Guarantee Replacement Industrial Program.

**grisaille**   Fancy "grizzled" dress fabric made in France. Poplin type in salt-and-pepper gray mixture with printed warp and coarse filling.

**Gro-Lon**   Trademark owned by Grove for its patented process on stretch torque yarn for hosiery.

**gros de londres**   Lightweight dress fabric, crisp and shiny, with alternating narrow and somewhat wider flat ribs. Sometimes described incorrectly as faille taffeta.

**grosgrain**   Closely woven ribbed fabric with pronounced crosswise cords, heavier and rounder than poplin.

**guanaco**   Rare fleece hair from scarce undomesticated animal, a progenitor of the llama and alpaca, larger than the alpaca or vicuna, smaller than the llama. Its fleece ranges from reddish brown to white, very fine and silky.

**guipure**   French for machine-made laces which have heavy gimp motifs connected by bars without mesh grounds.

# H

**habutai**   Soft, smooth, light, plain weave silk originally handwoven in Japan.

**hackle**   A board studded with long thin wire brushes used to comb and straighten flax fibers.

**hair**   Natural animal fiber other than sheep's wool or silk.

**haircloth**   Stiff, wiry fabric with horsehair filling used for interfacings.

**haircord**   English dress muslin made with thick warp cords. Also English bleached cotton fabric with colored warp cords. Similar to dimity but heavier.

**hand**   Touch, drape, weight of fall, or "handle" of a fabric.

**harlequin**   Diamond shape in distinct contrasting colors.

**harness**   The frame of a loom upon which the heddles used in weaving fabric are placed. Warp threads are drawn through the eye of the heddle, which moves up and down as the shuttle with filling yarn flies by. The movement of the heddle determines the pattern.

**Harris Tweed**   The British Board of Trade and the U.S. Federal Trade Commission recognize Harris Tweed as referring only to woolens handwoven on the islands of the Outer Hebrides off the coast of Scotland. This includes among others the island of Harris and Lewis. There are two types of Harris Tweed: 1. Fabric woven from hand-spun yarns. 2. Fabric woven from machine-spun yarns.

**Hazel**   Trademark owned by Sauquoit Fibers Co. for monofilament stretch yarns.

**heather mixture**   Combination of colors or fibers that suggests the color of Scottish heather.

**heat set**   To fix or set a yarn in crimped or textured form by use of heat.

**Heberlein** Trademark owned by Heberlein & Co., A.G. Wattwil, Switzerland, for a permanent crimp-finish process. Used by finishers under license.

**Heconda** Trademark owned by Heberlein & Co. for textured acetate or triacetate yarns or for plied yarns in blends with other synthetics.

**Hecospan** Trademark owned by Heberlein & Co. for Swiss core-twist yarn of crimped man-made fibers and spandex.

**Heeksuede** Trademark owned by Gebroeders Van Heek, N.V. Enschede, The Netherlands, for a substantial, closely woven cotton fabric with short brushed-suede surface.

**Helanca** Trademark owned by Heberlein & Co. for textured and stretch yarns of various types that meet firm's quality standards.

**Hemco** Trademark owned by Hemmerich for stretch nylon and polyester textured yarns. Also uses name *Hemlon*.

**hemp** Lustrous, durable, harsh bast fiber. Grows virtually all over the world, notably in Wisconsin, Kentucky, Italy, Russia. Steel gray to creamy white. Best grades are fine and white. Used chiefly for cordage, twine, sailcloth.

**henequen** A white-to-reddish-yellow, coarse, hard fiber obtained from the leaves of the henequen plant (*Agave fourcroydes*). Used mainly for cordage.

**Heplon** Trademark owned by Heplon Co. for nylon 6 and 66 yarns used mainly in carpet and industrial areas.

**herringbone** Broken-twill weave giving zigzag effect produced by alternating the direction of the twill, like the skeleton of a herring.

**Herculon**  Trademark owned by Hercules Inc. for continuous filament polypropylene olefin fibers and yarns.

**Hi-Narco**  Trademark owned by Beaunit Fibers for high-tenacity viscose fiber.

**hollow fibers**  Man-made fibers spun through spinneret with pronounced "C"-shaped holes. Filament resembles hollow macaroni. Man-made fibers are evaluated in various profiles such as "X," "Y," or even star shapes.

**homespun**  General terms for cloth handwoven at home instead of in a mill such as the linsey-woolsey, butternut, and coarse flannels woven on handlooms by early American settlers. Also coarse linens, cotton, drapery fabrics, etc.

**honan**  Wide silk fabric of good quality in pongee class made in Honan, China, now imitated elsewhere. Has lustrous occasional thick-thin thread effect both ways of the weave.

**honeycomb**  Weave with surface resembling the cells of a honeycomb.

**hopsacking**  An open, plied-yarn, coarse basket weave. Similar to sacking used to gather hops—hence the name.

**Hoskins mfs**  Trademark owned by Hoskins for metallic continuous filament stainless-steel alloy yarn. Used in tiny amounts to control static.

**houndstooth check**  Broken twill four-pointed star check.

**H.S.I.**  Trademark owned by Owens-Corning for fiberglas yarns or strands treated with resin for high strength.

**huarizo**  Hybrid member of the llama family (llama father and alpaca mother), bred for its fine fleece.

**hydrophilic fibers**  Fibers which absorb water readily, such as cotton, linen, or rayon.

**hydrophobic fibers**  Fibers which are non-absorptive and repel water. Nylon is an example.

**Hygram**  Trademark owned by Celanese Fibers Co. for high-tenacity viscose filament rayon yarn.

**Hytor**  Trademark owned by Atwater for a stretch-nylon torque-yarn process patented by Patentex, Inc.

# I

**Indian cotton**  India has grown cotton for thousands of years, ranks next to U.S. for quantity grown. Mostly short staple.

**insertion**  Narrow lace, binding, or embroidery with a plain edge on each side so that it may be set into a fabric.

**intarsia**  Colored pattern in a flat knitted fabric or sweater in which both sides of the fabric are alike. Generally geometrical.

**Intercel**  Trademark owned by Celanese Fibers Co. for acetate staple used for insulation.

**interfacing**  Woven and non-woven fabrics used between outer fabric and lining to reinforce or stiffen collars, cuffs, peplums, fronts, lapels, skirts, etc. Types include haircloth, canvas, plain cottons, crinolines, resin-stiffened materials, and non-wovens.

**interlining**  Layer of warm fabric, chamois, quilting, or other material between the outer cloth and lining of a garment.

**Interspan** Trademark owned by International Stretch Products for monofilament spandex fiber and yarn used mainly in foundations, swimwear, and industrial applications.

**intimate blend** The combining of two or more staple fibers in a spun yarn blended so intimately that individual fiber characteristics are dominated by the blend. Differs from a mixture where each component may retain its identity; e.g., heather mixtures.

**IRC Rayon** Trademark owned by American Cyanamid for filament viscose rayon staple fiber.

**Isralene** Trademark owned by Isranyl, Israeli yarn processor, for textured polyester filament yarn. Isralon and Isranyl are marks that denote nylon textured yarns.

**I.T.** Trademark owned by Americana Enka Corp. for improved tenacity rayon fiber . . . about 10% stronger than conventional rayon.

**iridescence** Changeable color effect usually obtained by contrasting colors in warp and filling yarns.

**Irish lace** Square mesh heavy crochet lace often ornamented with medallion, rose, or shamrock motifs. Edging has three-part scallop. "Irish" can be used for imports from Ireland only.

**Italvisca** Trademark owned by Snia Viscosa S.p.A. for a straw-like viscose rayon monofilament fiber. Produced in Italy; U.S. representative: Intercontinental Fibres, Inc.

**Ivorea** Trademark owned by Snia Viscosa S.p.A. for a dull viscose rayon filament yarn produced in Italy; U.S. representative: Intercontinental Fibres, Inc.

# J

**jacquard**  Woven-in pattern made by special looms which control individual weaving threads in warp to produce complicated patterns, more elaborate and expensive than dobbies. The jacquard machine—named for its French inventor, Jacquard—has also been adapted for fancy knitted patterns. Brocades and damasks are jacquards.

**jaspé**  Upholstery, drapery, or suiting fabric which has a series of faint stripes formed by light, medium, and dark threads of the same color.

**jersey**  Plain fabric knitted in tubular form on circular machine.

**Jetspun**  Trademark owned by American Enka Corp. for solution-dyed viscose rayon.

**jig-dyed**  Dyed in open width on a machine called a "jig." Cloth moves from one roll to another through the dye liquor until the desired shade is obtained.

**Joban**  Trademark owned by Chicopee Mfg. for non-flammable olefin fiber developed by Lumite Division and used for carpet backing licensed by Dawbarn.

**Jubilan**  Trademark owned by Nicholas-Dai Nippon Spinning Co., Ltd., for rayon fibers.

**Junron**  Trademark owned by Fujibo-Fuji Spinning Co., Ltd., for viscose rayon staple.

**jute**  Coarse, brown fiber from the stalk of a bast plant grown in India. Used mainly for burlap, cordage, and as a backing for rugs and carpets.

**Jutelac**  Trademark owned by Wellington for a synthetic backing yarn for woven carpet that simulates jute but is mildew proof and non-flammable.

# K

**Kanebo nylon**  Trademark owned by Japanese fiber-producing firm, Kanegafuchi Chemical Co. Ltd. Used mainly for Type 6 nylon filament yarn. Other Kanebo marks: *Kanelight* (olefin), *Kanelion* (rayon).

**Kanekalon**  Trademark owned by Japanese fiber firm Kanegafuchi Chemical Co. Ltd. for acrylic staple fiber. In textured form called *Highbulkee*.

**kasha**  Russian for "porridge." A flannel made of Tibetan goat hair slightly brushed with a crosswise streaked effect in darker hairs. Originated by Rodier in the 1920's.

**Kasymilon**  Trademark owned by Asahi Chemical Industry Co. Ltd. of Japan for acrylic staple and tow. Also called *Cashmilon*.

**kemp**  Short, wavy, coarse wool or hair fibers, usually white, which contain air spaces so that they resist dyeing and spinning. Used for carpets and decoration in costume fabrics.

**keratin**  The protein substance of which wool and hair are composed.

**kersey**  Woolen coating with shorter nap than beaver cloth and heavily fulled. (See beaver cloth; melton.)

**Keybak**  Trademark owned by Chicopee Manufacturing Corp. for non-woven porous interlining.

**khaki** Yellow-brown earth or dust colors, some with greenish tinge. Used mainly for uniforms, sportswear, and children's wear.

**kidde net** See power net.

**Kinkansei** Trademark owned by Toyobo-Toyo Spinning Co. Ltd. for high-tenacity viscose rayon filament yarn.

**kk-0001** Tentative designation for a Japanese graft fiber of 50% PVA and 50% PVC by Kojin.

**knit-de-knit** Unique yarn-texturizing method. Yarn is knitted into circular fabric steeve . . . then heat set . . . then unraveled, retaining its shape.

**knitting** Process of making fabric by interlocking series of loops of one or more yarns. Main types are jerseys (circular knits), and tricots (warp knits), and double knits.

**knop** Novelty yarns with pronounced knots of yarn of different color or material appearing at intervals. Also called *knotted* or *nub yarns*. Fabrics are described as "nubbed" or "knoppy."

**Kodacel** Trademark owned by Eastman Chemical Products for acetate-butyrate film for laminating to metallic foil for yarn.

**Kodel** Trademark owned by Eastman Chemical Products for polyester yarn and staple fiber.

**Kolorbon** Trademark owned by American Enka Corp. for solution-dyed crimped viscose rayon staple for carpets.

**Koratron** Trademark owned by Koratron Co. for durable-press process developed by Koret of California.

**Koroseal**  Trademark owned by Goodrich Rubber Co. for synthetic chemical product made of coal, limestone, and salt. Used to waterproof materials.

**Korspun**  Trademark owned by Caron, yarn processor, for core-spun yarn of man-made or natural fiber with spandex core.

**Krehalon**  Trademark owned by Kureha Chemical Industry Co. Ltd. in Japan for polyvinyl chloride "Vinyon" yarns. Another mark is *Kurehabo* (vinyl filament). Firm also produces nylon.

**Krispglo**  Trademark owned by American Enka Corp. for a flat rayon filament yarn that produces crisp linen-type fabrics.

**Kuralon**  Trademark owned by Kurashiki Rayon Co. Ltd., of Japan, for polyvinal alcohol "Vinal" fiber. Other Kurashiki marks: *Kuraray* (polyester), *Vinylon* (vinal).


# L


**lace**  Ornamental textile or trimming formed without the aid of a ground fabric, differing in this from embroidery. Real, or handmade, lace is made either by needle (point lace) or on a pillow by means of bobbins (pillow lace). Machine lace is measured according to the number of warp threads in an inch, as six-point, etc.

**lacquer prints**  Designs in which lustrous lacquer is used for colors.

**Lactron**  Trademark owned by UniRoyal for extruded latex (rubber) thread.

**Lambeth** Trademark owned by Lambeth for monofilament olefin fiber for rope and cordage.

**Lambette** Trademark owned by Associated Spinners for Turbo-processed acrylic high-bulk yarn.

**lamb's wool** First fleece taken from a sheep up to seven months old, having natural tapered fiber tip. Soft, superior spinning qualities over wools taken from older sheep that have been previously shorn and have fleece with blunt tips.

**lamé** Brocade with metal pattern or ground. Also plain metal fabric and fabric embroidered with metal.

**Lamé** Trademark owned by Standard Yarn Mills for non-tarnishable metallic, a combination of butyrate acetate laminated to aluminum on both sides with color injected in the adhesive.

**laminated** Term used for fabrics which have been joined together or bonded with foam, or other material.

**Lanaset** Trademark owned by American Cyanamid Co. for a resin treatment to control shrinkage of wool.

**Lanella** Trademark owned by Lanella Corp. for washable wool-and-cotton mixed fabrics made in Switzerland.

**Lanese** Trademark owned by Celanese Fibers Co. for acetate staple and spun yarns.

**Lastex** Trademark owned by UniRoyal for rubber strands covered with a variety of textile threads. With a spandex core, yarns are called *Lastex S.*

**lastocarb**  Generic name proposed to FTC for fiber of hydro-carbon chemistry, including natural rubber, polyisoprene, poly-butadiene, copolymers of dienes, hydrocarbons, etc.

**lastochlor**  Generic name proposed to FTC for fiber of poly-chloroprene or copolymer with at least 35% chloroprene.

**lastrile**  New generic term adopted by FTC to define fibers made from hydrocarbons, copolymers of acrylonitrile, or poly-chloroprene. Generally stretch fibers fall in this category. (See rubber.)

**latex**  The raw milky juice which is coagulated to form rubber.

**Laton**  Trademark owned by UniRoyal for rubber thread sheathed with natural or man-made fibers.

**lawn**  Sheer, plain cotton weave made of fine combed yarns, often in a high thread count.

**Leferon**  Trademark owned by Leon Ferenbach Inc. for crimped textured yarns.

**Lektroset**  Trademark owned by Midland-Ross Corp. for vis-cose rayon twist-set filament yarns.

**leno**  Open weave with mesh effect formed by warp yarns arranged in pairs so as to twist around each other between picks of filling yarns, as in marquisette, so holes won't slip. Made in patterned formations, such as stripes, squares, etc., as well as in allover effects.

**Lexan**  Trademark owned by General Electric for acrylic-latex polycarbonate fiber for space-age fabrics. Fiber still in experi-mental development stage.

**lille lace** Bobbin lace with fine mesh ground and pattern outlined with flat thread. Dots often scattered in design.

**linen** Yarn, thread, or fabric made from flax fibers. Term cannot be used except for natural flax fabrics.

**linen finish** Finish on fabrics not made of flax to make them look like linen.

**Lintella** Trademark owned by Beaunit Fibers for thick-and-thin viscose rayon filament yarn.

**Lirelle** Trademark owned by Courtaulds North America for high-modulus viscose rayon staple in approved fabrics. (See Moynel.)

**lisle** Hard twisted, long-staple, combed cotton thread, treated with gas to give lustrous effect and soft hand to hosiery and knitted underwear.

**Livolon** Trademark owned by Patentex Inc. for nylon stretch yarn for hosiery and pantyhose. Process licensed to Chadbourne.

**llama** Soft, strong underfleece of the llama, a South American animal similar to but smaller than a camel. Four distinct types in family: llama, alpaca, guanaco, vicuna. Usually found in Peru and Bolivia. Two hybrid types huarizo (llama father, alpaca mother) and paco-llama (alpaca father, llama mother).

**Lock-Lined** Trademark owned by Lock-Line Inc. for process for bonding fabrics permanently. Firm licenses mark and process.

**loden cloth** Coating of fleecy type woven in Tyrolese area of Austria and Germany from wool of coarser grades that retains some grease, thereby having natural water repellency. Usually a deep soft wood green.

**Loftura** Trademark owned by Tennessee Eastman Co. for bulked-filament acetate yarns with long slubs up to four inches.

**Loktuft** Trademark owned by Phillips for non-woven carpet backing made of Marvess olefin fiber. Used for tufted and flocked carpeting.

**London shrinkage** Method of shrinking by cold-water bath, followed by drying and pressing.

**longcloth** Another name for nainsook, lightweight cotton of the lawn type, usually combed and slightly mercerized.

**Long Type "A" Slub** Trademark owned by Beaunit Fibers for rayon yarn with long, parallel, non-entangled slubs.

**loom** A weaving machine for producing textiles by interlacing warp and filling yarns in perpendicular fashion.

**Loop-Spun** Trademark owned by Lohrke Textiles Inc. for a specialty spun yarn of 65% Kodel polyester and 35% Verel modacrylic. Another Lohrke specialty spun yarn is *Lortweed*.

**Lorette** Trademark owned by Deering Milliken for cloth of 55/45 Orlon and wool blend.

**Lorganza** Trademark owned by Bianchini, Ferier Inc. for a crisp sheer silk organdy.

**Lowland** Trademark owned by American Enka Corp. to identify nylon, rayon, and polyester fibers and yarns produced at its Lowland, Tenn., plant and not identified with individual marks.

**Lurex** Trademark owned by Dow Badische Co. for wide variety of non-tarnishable aluminum metallic yarns.

**Lusterella**   Trademark owned by William Heller Inc. for a silky textured acetate yarn.

**Lusterlite**   Trademark owned by Dawbarn Division, W. R. Grace, for a decorative polypropylene olefin yarn.

**Lus-Trus**   Trademark owned by Southern Lus-Trus for olefin monofilament fiber for upholstery fabrics, ropes, and webbing.

**Lycra**   Trademark owned by Du Pont for polyurethane multifilament spandex elastomer. The fused multifilaments in a bundle form a monofilament yarn that stretches and snaps back into place like rubber. Launched in 1958 as Fiber K.

**lyons velvet**   A rather stiff, crisp tailoring velvet with a short dense erect pile.

## M

**Madagascar**   Trademark owned by McCampbell & Co. Inc. for cotton fabric woven and finished to simulate straw.

**Madagascar lace**   Lace of thread twisted into loops and scallops; made by natives of Madagascar.

**Madara Set**   Trademark owned by Madison Throwing Co. for textured polyester yarn.

**madras**   Fine cotton shirting fabric with woven pattern, dobby or jacquard stripe, cord, or check effect. The stripe, cord, or check may be same color or contrasting. *India madras:* coarse spun cotton made in Madras, India, in colorful plaids; the colors bleed when washed. (See bleeding.)

**Magic Spun**   Trademark owned by United Yarn Products Co. for a variety of spun yarns of man-made fibers.

**Magiloft**   Trademark owned by Madison Throwing Co. for stretch and textured filament yarns of man-made fibers.

**Malimo**   Textile-making machine developed in East Germany that neither knits nor weaves, but forms fabrics at extremely high speeds by using three sets of yarns. It takes a creel of warp yarns, lays filling yarns across them, stitches the whole thing together with a third set of yarns.

**malines or Mechlin lace**   Bobbin lace with design outlined by a lustrous thread on a fine six-sided mesh ground which itself is known as *malines* or *tulle.*

**Malora**   Trademark owned by Malina Co. for butyrate acetate made in slit form like metal yarn but without metal.

**Malora with Mylar**   Trademark owned by Malina Co. for polyester-coated metallic yarns. Metallic polyester-wound yarn is trademarked *Malora with Mylar Foil.*

**marl**   Two yarns of different colors or kinds twisted around each other.

**Marlene**   Trademark owned by Sauquoit Fibers Co. for modified stretch yarns.

**Marlex 50**   Trademark owned by Phillips Fibers for a polyethylene resin to make olefin fibers.

**marocain crepe**   Heavy crepe with coarse filling giving cross-ribbed effect; a heavy relative of canton crepe.

**marquisette**   Transparent open-mesh leno weave.

**Marshal-Ized**   Trademark owned by Glenn of America, yarn spinner, for Turbo-processed fine-denier Orlon filament yarn.

**Marvess**   Trademark owned by Phillips Fibers for its olefin fiber.

**matelassé** Fancy weave, usually jacquard, with raised patterns that look quilted, wadded, puckered, blistered, etc. Net-like back holds it in shape. Types may be firm like taffetas or soft and crepe-like.

**Matesa** Trademark owned by Beaunit Fibers for dull-filament cuprammonium rayon yarn.

**matte jersey** Dull tricot made of fine crepe yarns.

**Mazet** Trademark owned by Deering Milliken for 100% Turbo Orlon-acrylic yarn used in sweaters, etc.

**Measle** Trademark owned by Beaunit Fibers for rayon yarn with part tight and part loose filaments.

**meisen** Plain silk weave from Japan with fancy variations of blurry crosses in white or color obtained by hand-coloring small areas of both warp and filling yarns before weaving.

**Melofil** Trademark owned by Duplan Corp. for stretch, bulked, or crimped nylon or polyester yarn.

**melton** Coating with all-wool or cotton warp and woolen weft; the face is napped carefully, raising the nap straight, to show the weave clearly. Made originally in Melton, England. (See beaver cloth; kersey.)

**Meraklon** Trademark owned by Montecatini So. Gen., of Italy, for olefin fiber (polypropylene).

**mercerizing** Finish named for originator, John Mercer. Used on cotton yarns and fabrics to increase luster and to improve stretch and dyeability. Treatment consists of impregnating fabrics with cold concentrated sodium hydroxide solution. Best results are obtained on combed goods; widely used for knitted fabrics, and on wool for high luster and strength.

**merino** 1. Wool from the Merino sheep which makes fine, soft fabrics resembling cashmere. Often mixed with silk and cotton. 2. In knit underwear, garments made from yarns spun from a mixture of cotton and wool.

**mesh** Any fabric, knitted or woven, with an open texture, fine or coarse.

**Metalastic** Trademark owned by Metlon Corp. for laminated types of metallic yarns.

**metallic** Generic term established by Federal Trade Commission for a manufactured fiber composed of plastic-coated metal, metal-coated plastic, or a core completely covered by metal.

**Metlon** Trademark owned by Metlon Corp. for a non-tarnishable metallic yarn produced by laminating bright aluminum foil between two plies of plastic film. When high-tenacity metallic yarns are used with Mylar polyester laminate the trademark is called *Metlon H.T. Mylar*. Polyester-coated metal yarn is called *Metlon-with-Mylar*.

**Micro-Stretch** A patented development of Radunder & Co. AG, of Horne, Switzerland, that improves tensile strength of cotton fabrics and increases width. Sanforized Co., a division of Cluett Peabody & Co., is world-wide licensing and technical service agent.

**Microtex** Trademark owned by Joseph Bancroft and licensed to converters for finished fabrics made on microcreper machine. It's a method for texturizing fabric instead of yarn. In approved garments the term *Bandura* may be used.

**milan lace** Bobbin lace, similar to Belgian, net ground with designs formed of tape or braid, in scroll or floral motifs.

**Milanese** A type of warp knit with pronounced diagonal effect.

**mildew-resistant fabric**  Fabric treated to resist growth of mildew or mold.

**Milium**  Registered trademark of Deering Milliken for insulating fabrics utilizing reflective materials for women's wear, men's wear, draperies, window shades, and home-furnishings fabrics.

**Mitin**  Trademark owned by Geigy Co. Inc. for a moth-repellent finish for woolens and precious hair fabrics such as cashmere and vicuna.

**modacrylic**  Generic name established by the Federal Trade Commission for "a manufactured fiber in which the fiber-forming substance is any long-chain synthetic polymer composed of less than 85% but at least 35% by weight of acrylonitrile units, except when it qualifies as rubber."

**Modulized**  Trademark owned by Midland-Ross for fabrics made of Nupron high-wet-modulus rayon staple.

**modulus**  Positive quantity, numerical or physical, that expresses the measure of elasticity. That is, the amount of stretch and return. Important to the design of foundations, swimwear, and other elastic fabric functions.

**mogador**  Originally tie silk, now also of man-made fibers. Resembles fine faille.

**mohair**  Long, straight fiber from the Angora goat. From four to 12 inches long, comparatively coarse, silky, very lightweight, fluffs up fabrics.

**moiré**  Finish or process generally applied to fabrics in which the warp has yarn of harder twist than the filling. The moiré effect resembles water ripples, is produced by engraved rollers, heat, pressure, steam, and chemicals.

**moleskin** Heavy filling-faced carded-cotton cloth with low-angle right twill. Often napped and sheared to give suede effect.

**momme** Japanese unit of weight (equal to 3.75 grams) used to describe the weight of silk fabrics. The higher the momme, the heavier the fabric.

**monk's cloth** Heavy basket weave for couch covers, draperies, and furniture.

**monofilament** Any single filament of sufficient size and strength to function as a yarn in normal textile operations.

**Monosheer** Trademark owned by American Enka Corp. for a nylon hosiery yarn.

**Monostretch** Trademark owned by United Elastic Corp. for polypropylene monofilament yarns and narrow elastics.

**moratronic** A patterned fabric, most often polyester double-knit, made on a German knitting machine of the same name. It is capable of turning out larger patterns than comparable jacquard knitting machines.

**mordant** A metallic salt used for fixing dyes on fibers or fabrics.

**moss, mossy crepes** Various crepes constructed and finished to have a mossy look.

**motif** Salient feature or subject of a composition or work. In fabrics, the dominant figure or effect in a woven or printed pattern.

**mourning crepe** Dull semi-sheer crepe which often has a moiré effect. Often with a pronounced crepon or lengthwise crinkle.

**mousseline**  Lightweight crisp sheer finer than muslin. Ordinarily used in connection with fiber name; for example, "mousseline de soie."

**Moynel**  Trademark owned by Courtaulds, now replaced by *Lirelle.*

**M.P.**  Trademark owned by Leon-Ferenbach for textured-nylon carpet yarn.

**muga**  One of the best wild silks, grown in India; means "light brown."

**Multi-Cupioni**  Trademark owned by Beaunit Fibers for doupion-type thick-and-thin rayon yarn with entangled slubs.

**multifilament**  Denotes yarns made of many fiber strands or filaments. Some fibers are spun in very fine filament form. These are then plied or fused together.

**Multi-Strata Slub**  Trademark owned by Beaunit Fibers for rayon yarns with torpedo-shaped slubs.

**muslin**  Generic term for wide variety of cotton fabrics ranging from thin batiste and nainsook to longcloth, percale, and heavy sheeting.

**Mylar polyester**  Trademark owned by Du Pont for a durable transparent water-repellent polyester film. One of its uses is in laminating aluminum metal yarns.

**Mylast**  Trademark owned by Meyers for crimp-type textured thermoplastic yarns for sweaters, carpets, tufted or woven goods, and upholstery.

**nacré velvet** Velvet with back of one color and pile of another, giving a changeable, pearly appearance (nacré). Also glacé velvet similarly made to get iridescent effect.

**nainsook** Lightweight cotton cloth of lawn type, usually combed, finished with slight mercerized luster. (See lawn.)

**Nantuck** Trademark owned by Du Pont for blended yarns of conventional and bicomponent Orlon fibers.

**napped** Various fabrics finished with a brushing that raises the surfaces.

**Narco** Trademark owned by Beaunit Fibers for continuous filament viscose rayon fiber.

**Narcon** Trademark owned by Beaunit Fibers for high-strength viscose rayon staple.

**Narcrest** Trademark owned by Beaunit Fibers for bulked viscose rayon filament yarns.

**Narene** Trademark owned by Beaunit Fibers for viscose rayon filament yarns.

**Naticetta** Trademark owned by National Spinning for textured Antron yarns.

**needlepoint** Simple stitch embroidery completely covering mesh or canvas grounds. Variations are *gros point* (coarse) and *petit point* (fine).

**Neochrome**   Trademark owned by Courtaulds for producer-dyed acrylic fiber.

**net**   Fabric of thread or twine made in open hexagonal mesh. Mostly made on bobbinet lace machine, but also on knitting machine. Ranges from tulle to fishing nets.

**Never-Press**   Trademark owned by Wamsutta Mills, Division of M. Lowenstein, for durable-press process.

**Newbray**   Trademark owned by Mohasco for rayon filament yarn.

**ninon**   A sheer crisp fabric in plain weave heavier than chiffon used for evening wear, curtains, lingerie, etc.

**noil**   Short fibers removed in combing and spun into yarn, used for roughish texture, nubbed surface, novelty effect.

**Nomelle**   Trademark owned by Du Pont for certification of yarns of super-soft Orlon acrylic.

**Nomex**   Trademark owned by Du Pont for HT-1 fiber, a high-temperature heat-resistant nylon filament or staple fiber that can withstand heat up to 1,000°F.

**non-woven**   Neither woven, knitted, nor spun. A material made of fibers in a web or mat held together by a bonding agent.

**Norane**   Trademark owned by Warwick Chemical Co., division of Sun Chemical Corp., for water-repellent finish.

**nottingham**   Flat lace originally machine-made in Nottingham, England. Now used as name for lace made anywhere on nottingham-type machine.

**N.P.I.** The number of *needles per inch* in the cylinder or needle bed in a knitting frame. Sometimes referred to as *cut*.

**nubbed fabric** Fabric decorated with novelty yarn containing slubs, knots, beads, or lumps.

**Nubbi** Trademark owned by Beaunit Fibers for viscose rayon filament yarn.

**Nub-Lite** Trademark owned by Beaunit Fibers for nubby thick-and-thin cuprammonium rayon filament fiber with short slubs.

**Numa** Trademark owned by Ameliotex Inc. for a multi-filament spandex fiber in round profile.

**nun's veiling** Lightweight, sheer, plain weave similar to challis.

**Nupron** Trademark owned by American Cyanamid for rayon fabrics made of high-modulus staple fiber.

**Nyacry** Trademark owned by Blackwelder to identify bulked-textured yarns of nylon and acrylic.

**Nyfoyle** Trademark owned by Aberfoyle Mfg. Co. for a processed yarn of nylon and other fibers.

**Nyflock** Trademark owned by Precision Fibers for flock of man-made fibers.

**nylon** Generic name for "a manufactured fiber in which the fiber-forming substance is any long-chain synthetic polyamide having recurring amide groups as an integral part of the polymer chain."

**Nypel** Trademark owned by Nypel Corp. for monofilament nylon and olefin fibers and fabrics.

**Nytelle** Trademark owned by Firestone for fine-denier filament nylon.

**nytril** Generic name adopted by the Federal Trade Commission for "a manufactured fiber containing at least 85% of a long-chain polymer of vinylidene dinitrile where the vinylidene dinitrile content is no less than every other unit in the polymer chain."

# O

**olefin** Generic name for "a manufactured fiber in which the fiber-forming substance is any long-chain synthetic polymer composed of at least 85% by weight of ethylene, propylene, or other olefin units except amorphous (non-crystalline) polyolefins qualifying as rubber." Basic raw materials are petroleum by-products.

**Olefini** Trademark owned by Roselon, yarn processor, for textured yarn made via textralized Ban-Lon process for hosiery.

**oligomers** Chemical generic term for defining intermediate substances used in fiber-making that fall between monomers and polymers.

**Olympia-Set** Trademark owned by Olympia, yarn processors, for textured set filament yarns of polyester made via ARCT process.

**ombré** French for shaded or graduated (degradé) color ranging from light to dark tones, such as cream to brown; also for tones that shade from one color into another.

**Ondelette** Trademark owned by Beaunit Fibers for random-slubbed rayon yarn.

**ondulé**  Wavy effect in a fabric achieved by weaving.

**organdy**  Sheer, crisp, plain cotton weave made of fine combed yarns.

**organza**  French for transparent crisp silk organdy.

**organzine**  A fine yarn of best quality silk that consists of two or three filaments twisted together. Also applied to some manufactured yarns.

**Orlon**  Trademark owned by Du Pont for acrylic staple fiber.

**Orlon Sayelle**  Trademark owned by Du Pont for acrylic staple fiber with permanent reversible crimp.

**Orofil**  Trademark owned by Rohm & Haas for high-modulus elastomeric cut monofilament fiber—not spandex—classified as rubber.

**Ortalion**  Trademark owned by Beaunit Fibers for texturized nylon yarn produced in Italy.

**ottoman**  Heavyweight fabric with pronounced crosswise rounded ribs, often padded. Similar to faille or bengaline but with heavier ribs.

**overcheck**  One check of different size or color superimposed upon another.

**overplaid**  Double plaid in which weave or, more often, color effect is arranged in blocks of the same or different sizes, one over the other.

**oxford**  Stout shirting, finished with a silk luster, chiefly in plain or fancy basket weaves, with narrow colored warp stripes. Oxford also describes a dark grayish-looking color or fabric of mixed black and white yarns.

**oxidative coupling**   An experimental process for a new technique of fiber-making currently under investigation by General Electric and American Enka.


# P


**paillette**   French for "sequin." Generally paillettes are somewhat larger than sequins and shaped differently. The former have holes in tops and hang loosely; the latter generally have center holes and are sewn firmly to cloth.

**paisley**   Decorative multicolored design, woven or printed, also called *cashmere*. Originally taken from the genuine cashmere shawls of India by shawl weavers in Paisley, Scotland. Design has typical Indian palm or cone figures and elaborate symmetrical detail.

**panama**   Plain woven hopsacking of coarse-yarn basket weave, plain or in two colors, producing effect similar to texture of panama hats.

**panné**   Velvet with pile pressed flat in one direction; very lustrous.

**Parfé**   Trademark owned by Beaunit Fibers for filament rayon yarn with intermittently spaced dyed colors.

**passementerie**   General term (French) applied to heavy lacy edgings and trimmings of gimp, cord, beads, etc.

**Patlon**   Trademark owned by Patchogue-Plymouth for monofilament olefin carpet yarns that have been fibrillated.

**peau de soie**   French (meaning "skin of silk") for soft closely woven satin with very compact face of mellow luster.

**pebble** Irregular or rough surface with pebbly look, as in a pebble crepe.

**Pellon** Trademark owned by Pellon Corp. of America for non-woven interfacings in various weights. Used for under-shaping of coats, suits, and dresses, petticoats; stiffening fronts, collars, cuffs, etc.

**percale** Printed or plain cotton sheeting usually converted from better combed constructions, such as 80x80 (80 square). Cheaper qualities may be carded cottons. "Eighty square" means 160 threads to the square inch, adding those in each direction.

**permanent finish** Fabric treatment of various kinds to improve glaze, hand, or performance of fabrics. These finishes are durable in laundering and usually effective for the normal use-life of the fabric.

**Permanese** Trademark owned by Celanese Fibers Co. for solution-dyed acetate filament yarn made in Mexico.

**Permel Plus** Trademark owned by American Cyanamid Co. for washable, water-repellent process, also crease and soil resistant. Firm uses trademark *Permel* as the first component of various other trade names for finishes as well as this one.

**Pesanté** Trademark owned by Saks Fifth Avenue for heavy rustic-looking doupion silk suitings imported from Italy.

**Pharr-Mist** Trademark owned by Pharr, yarn processor, for Turbo-processed acrylic spun yarn.

**Phillips 66** Trademark owned by Fibers International for fine-denier nylon filament yarn produced in Puerto Rico.

**photographic prints** Made with photoengraved rollers that transfer photographs to cloth. Several processes, all adapted from color printing on paper.

**pick**  One thread of warp or filling.

**pick-and-pick**  One type of crosswise thread alternated with another, such as cotton or acetate alternated with rubber yarn in corset and bathing-suit fabrics.

**picot**  Decorative woven edge of tiny loops in the selvages of ribbon, lace, or fabric. Picot effects may also be obtained by machine hemstitching cut through the center.

**piece dying**  Material dyed in the piece after weaving.

**pigment prints**  Made with insoluble pigment mixed with a binder and thickener to form the printing paste.

**pile fabric**  Fabric with cut or uncut loops which stand up densely on the surface. Not to be confused with napped fabrics, which have brushed surfaces. Velvets, plushes, velveteens, and corduroys are pile fabrics; also fur imitations described as "deep pile."

**pilling**  The formation of little fuzzy balls on a fabric surface caused by the rubbing off of loose ends of fiber too long or strong to break away entirely.

**pima cotton**  Fine-quality, long-staple cotton fiber grown in Pima, Arizona, developed from Egyptian cotton seed. Now grown in other far western states, too. Used for fine-combed cottons, often mercerized. (See Supima.)

**pincheck**  Very tiny check, usually shepherd or crow's foot.

**piqué**  Fabric with raised lengthwise cords, welts, or wales in various plain and patterned effects, such as fine, medium, and heavy wales, honeycomb, waffle, diamond, and birdseye.

**plaid**  Pattern of colored stripes or bars crossing each other at right angles.

**plied-yarn fabrics**  Cloths made of varied or similar yarns twisted together in two-ply, three-ply, four-ply, etc., constructions.

**plissé**  Thin cotton fabric, soft or crisp, with puckered stripes or patterns in allover blister effect. Obtained either by weaving with yarns having different degrees of shrinkage in finishing or by chemical treatment.

**plush**  Warp pile fabric with silk or wool pile longer than that of velvet.

**Plustretch**  Trademark owned by J. P. Stevens for core-spun stretch hosiery yarn.

**ply yarn**  Yarn made by twisting together two or more single yarns in one operation.

**point d'esprit**  Bobbin cotton net with small square dots scattered on its surface.

**point de paris**  Bobbin lace with six-sided mesh ground design in clothlike texture, usually outlined with a heavy cord.

**Poliafil**  Trademark owned by Sauquoit for fine-denier nylon filament yarn.

**polyamide**  Compounds formed by polymerization of amino acids or by condensation of diamines with dicarboxylic acids. Basic fiber-forming substances for nylon.

**Poly-Bac**  Trademark owned by Patchogue-Plymouth for woven carpet backing of olefin fiber.

**Polycrest**  Trademark owned by UniRoyal for olefin fiber used in carpets.

**polyester**   Generic term for a manufactured fiber in which the fiber-forming substance is any long-chain synthetic polymer composed of at least 85% by weight of an ester of dihydric alcohol and terephthalic acid.

**Polyglas**   Trademark owned by Goodyear for polyester tire cord. No apparel applications.

**Polykor**   Trademark owned by Patchogue-Plymouth for olefin yarns for woven carpet backings.

**Polyloom**   Trademark owned by Chevron for fibrillated split-film olefin carpet fiber.

**polymer**   A synthetic material from which fibers are formed. Usually composed of large molecules formed by the union of single molecules (monomers) with each other.

**Polynosic**   Trademark owned by American Enka Corp. for high-modulus dimensionally stable modified viscose rayon staple.

**polypropylene**   Basic fiber-forming substance for an olefin fiber.

**pongee**   Plain-woven, lightweight or medium-weight fabric made from wild silk. Almost always pale or dark tan, but now also sometimes printed, bleached, and dyed in colors.

**poodle cloth**   Loopy bouclé or knotted yarn cloth that looks like the coat of a French poodle. Originally wool, also made of various fibers and mixtures in knitted as well as woven versions.

**poplin**   Term applied to fabrics with fine imbedded rib running from selvage to selvage.

**Popparoni**   Trademark owned by Glen Raven for acetate knit-de-knit textured yarn.

**post-curing** Technique for imparting durable press that requires baking made-up goods in ovens at predetermined temperature and time to cure fabrics that have been pre-treated with special resins. Most common and accepted technique used with polyester and cotton blends. (See durable press.)

**poult de soie** Silk fabric in plain weave with heavy filling strands forming cross ribs. Sometimes called *faille taffeta*.

**power net** 1. Thin rubber-containing net made on bobbinette machine for girdles; stretches in all directions. 2. Less expensive knitted net made on a Kidde or raschel machine; stretches in all directions. 3. Inexpensive leno weave that usually stretches in one direction only.

**pre-curing** Technique for imparting durable press by treating fabrics with special resins, then curing same on goods. Does not require oven after-treatment of DP apparel. Resins may be set via use of high-temperature hot-head presses alone, which serve to impart the DP qualities to a garment. (See durable press.)

**printing** Process of producing designs of one or more colors on a fabric. There are several methods, such as roller, block, screen, etc., and several color techniques, such as direct, discharge, and resist. Block and screen prints are generally more expensive than roller prints. (See application printing.)

**producer-textured yarns** General term for yarns textured by fiber producers rather than by throwsters.

**Proex** Trademark owned by Polymers for x-profile olefin monofilament yarns for industrial products. No apparel applications.

**Pro-Fax** Trademark owned by Hercules for polypropylene resins used in Herculon olefin fiber production.

**profile**   Term used to describe shape of a cross-section of a fiber filament. Can be round, dogbone, bilobal, pentalobal, x-shaped, y-shaped, etc.

**puckered cloths**   Term adopted for pebbled crimped plissé or cockled nylon cloths. Trade calls all "puckers."

**Puffee**   Trademark owned by Pocasset for Turbo-processed Orlon yarn processed by Glenn of America.


# Q

**Qiana**   Trademark owned by Du Pont for new luxury silk-like nylon fiber. Differs from conventional nylon 6 in its molecular structure and chemical linkage. Introduced in 1967. Has distinctive luster, dry soft hand, and high wrinkle resistance.

**Qiviut**   Underwool of the domesticated musk ox. Considered the rarest and most luxurious wool fiber in the world. First herd was established at College, Alaska, in cooperation with the University of Alaska under a grant from the Kellogg Foundation. That herd now numbers 64 animals. Other herds have been established in Quebec and Alaska, with the Mekoryuk Eskimo women now knitting scarves from these fine wools. One bull sheds up to six pounds of qiviut fiber each year and cows somewhat less. Fleece is not shorn from the musk ox but is shed naturally and removed from the guard hairs as it becomes visible. In years to come when fiber is available in commercial quantities it is expected to run somewhere between $35 and $50 per pound.

**quartz fibers**   Fibers produced by General Electric Co. based on quartz silica filaments for specialized application in radomes, etc. No apparel uses.

**quill**  A tapered wooden cone on which filling yarn is wound preparatory to weaving. Sometimes, the package of yarn itself.

**Quilticel**  Trademark owned by Celanese Fibers Co. for bonded acetate staple batting used for insulation. When used in baby buntings is called *Quiltron*.

**quilting**  Two or more layers of cloth with padding between stitched through by hand, machine, or chemical methods, usually in a pattern such as diamonds, scrolls, etc.

**Quintess**  Trademark owned by Phillips Fibers for polyester staple and filament yarns.

**Qulon**  Merchandising trademark of Beaunit Fibers for approved end products of nylon 66 used in carpets, home furnishings, and industrial applications.

## R

**"R"**  Trademark owned by Owens-Corning for high-tensile-strength glass fiber.

**rabbit hair**  Hair from the common rabbit or hare. Usually light brown. Occasionally blended in various weaves and knits for softness or to obtain some special effect.

**radium**  Smooth, soft-lustered plain-weave silk or rayon fabric similar to habutai.

**radzimir**  Also spelled "rhadzimir." Fine lustrous silk fabric with embedded cross-ribs. Softer, less crisp, and duller than faille taffeta.

**ramie**   Fiber from the ramie plant. Strong, lustrous, similar to flax but more brittle. Chiefly for table linen.

**raschel**   Warpknit, similar to tricot, but coarser. Made in wide variety of patterns including lace and net. Named for creator of the machine.

**ratiné**   Knotty nubby yarn used to make a fancy "plain" fabric. Also, loose plain-woven cloth made of ratiné yarns in one or both directions. Also called *éponge, frisé,* and *sponge cloth.*

**rattail**   Narrow round soutache braid.

**Ravenna**   Trademark owned by Glen Raven for new textured-yarn process.

**raw silk**   Silk reeled from cocoons before natural gum is removed.

**Rayflex**   Trademark owned by the American Viscose Division of FMC for high-strength continuous filament viscose rayon yarn.

**rayon**   A generic name for man-made fibers, monofilaments, and continuous filaments, made from regenerated cellulose. Fibers produced by both viscose and cuprammonium process are classified as rayon.

**rayonné**   French derivation; generic term for viscose rayon staple.

**reactive dyes**   Classes of dyes that react chemically with the molecules of the fiber, resulting in unusually fast, brilliant colors.

**Recall**   Trademark owned by Celanese Fibers Co., yarn processor, for nylon filament stretch yarn made via ARCT process.

**reeling**  Unwinding single silk filaments from unbroken co-coons.

**Reemay**  Trademark owned by Du Pont for spunbonded poly-ester filaments bonded in random fashion into a sheet structure or fabric.

**Reevaire**  Trademark owned by Reeves Bros. Inc. for a breath-able rainwear finish.

**Refrasil**  Trademark owned by H. I. Thompson Fiber Glass Co. for a fused silica fiber.

**renaissance lace**  Woven tape motifs joined by a variety of flat stitches forming lace.

**rep, repp**  Either spelling correct. Fabrics characterized by dis-tinct, round, padded ribs running from selvage to selvage.

**reprocessed wool**  Yarn made from wool that has been woven, knitted, or felted into a wool product which, without ever hav-ing been used, has been returned to a fibrous state. Cloth cut-tings, for example, when reduced to a fibrous state become reprocessed wool.

**resilience**  The property of a textile material to recover from a deformed state. In carpeting, loosely defined as crushability.

**resist dyeing**  Method of treating yarn or cloth so that in dye-ing the treated parts do not absorb the dyestuff.

**resist prints**  Made by first printing the designs using a sub-stance that resists dyestuffs. Fabric is then piece dyed to obtain the wanted color in the untreated portion.

**retting**  The soaking of flax plant to loosen fiber from stalk.

**reverse twill weave** Term sometimes applied to patterned twill weaves in which both right- and left-hand twills are used; for example, broken and pointed twill.

**Reymet** Trademark owned by Reynolds Metals Co. for metallic fiber of Mylar polyester film laminated to aluminum foil and to another sheet of Mylar film. Other types of film may be used: acetate, butyrate, cellophane.

**Rheeflex** Trademark owned by Rohm & Haas for uncovered rubber and synthetic yarns.

**Rhodia** Trademark owned by Rhodiaceta, S.A., for acetate yarn products. French.

**Rhodianese** Trademark owned by Rhodia for combination knitting yarns blended of textured acetate and rayon.

**Rhovyl** Trademark owned by Societe Rhovyl S.A. for polyvinyl chloride filament yarn and staple. French. Firm proposes adoption of term *chlorofibre* as generic classification.

**rib** Usually a straight raised cord, formed by heavy thread, lengthwise, crosswise, or diagonal. Many knitted fabrics are ribbed lengthwise.

**ribbon** Narrow woven fabric with woven selvage for trimming or decoration.

**ribbon, cut edge** Certain cheap ribbons, especially velvet or acetate satin, made from wide fabric, cut into narrow strips, the raw edge fused in the cutting.

**rickrack** Form of decorative flat braid in wavy chevron form made of cotton, rayon, silk, metal, etc.

**Rigmel** Trademark owned by Bradford Dyeing Association for shrinkage process which also gives luster and soft touch to

**100**

cotton shirting and dress fabrics. Will not shrink more than 1% in length or width.

**Rocel**   Trademark owned by Roselon, yarn processor, for textured filament nylon yarn.

**roller prints**   Machine made, using engraved copper rollers, one for each color in the pattern (each with its own color trough), mounted behind the cylinder. Cloth passes between rollers and the cylinder, where dye is picked up.

**Romaine Crepe**   Trademark owned by Bianchini Ferier for a heavy sheer basket-weave crepe.

**Rosefrost**   Trademark owned by Roselon, yarn processor, for textured nylon yarns. Other marks include *Roselo, Roselon,* and *Rosette.*

**rose point**   Venice lace worked in relief. Also known as *gros point* or *venetian rose point.*

**Rotofil**   Designation used by Du Pont for yarns of staple fibers bound together by surface fibers wrapped around the yarn bundle. Introduced in 1970.

**Rotoset**   Designation used by Du Pont for multifilament yarns treated by patented process to entwine or interlace filaments, eliminating need for yarn twisting.

**Rovanna**   Trademark owned by Dow Chemical Co. for flat monofilament saran in solution-dyed colors.

**rubber**   New generic definition revised by Federal Trade Commission in February 1966 terms rubber "a fiber in which the fiber-forming substance is composed of natural or synthetic rubber, including the following categories:
"(1) A fiber in which the fiber-forming substance in a hydrocarbon such as natural rubber, polyisoprene, polybutadiene,

copolymers of dienes and hydrocarbons or amorphous (non-crystalline) polyolefins.

"(2) A fiber in which the fiber-forming substance is a copolymer of acrylonitrile and a diene (such as butadiene) composed of not more than 50% but at least 10% by weight of acrylonitrile units. The term 'lastrile' may be used as a generic description for fibers falling in this category.

"(3) A fiber in which the fiber-forming substance is a polychloroprene or a copolymer of chloroprene in which at least 35% by weight of fiber-forming substance is composed of chloroprene units."

**Rucaire**   Trademark owned by Hooker Chemical for polyurethane materials made from polyester substrates.

**Ruvea**   Trademark owned by Du Pont for nylon ribbon yarn used in luggage, shoes, and golf bags. No apparel application.

## S

**"S"**   Trademark owned by Owens-Corning for high-strength glass fiber.

**"S" twist**   See torque yarns.

**Saaba**   Trademark owned by Leesona Corp. for a modified bulked textured stretch yarn made by reprocessing Superloft or Fluflon stretch yarn.

**Sag-No-Mor**   Trademark owned by the Wyner Division of Ames Textile Co. for a worsted jersey designed to keep from sagging or stretching.

**sailcloth**   Heavy, strong canvas weave. Made in many qualities, widths, and fibers.

**sand crepe**   Crepe with grainy or sandy surface. Has "dry" touch.

**Sanforized**   Trademark owned by Cluett, Peabody & Co. for fabrics processed by machine so that residual shrinkage will not exceed 1% in either direction. The firm licenses its process in the U.S. and abroad under a quality-control program.

**Sanforized-Plus**   Trademark owned by Cluett, Peabody & Co. for a rigid wash-wear quality performance. Fabrics are tested by a special electronic smoothness evaluator for shrinkage, crease recovery, tensile strength, and tear strength.

**saponification**   Treatment of acetate with alkalies that changes fiber surface to allow use of direct dyes, such as those used on cottons and viscose.

**saran**   Generic name for man-made fibers composed of co-polymers of vinylidene and vinyl chlorides.

**Sarille**   Trademark owned by Courtaulds for producer-textured modified rayon staple.

**sateen**   Cotton cloth made in a satin weave. Usually mercer-ized, often treated with high-luster and crease-resistant finishes.

**satin**   Fabric with yarn floated to the surface to give lustrous face. Many varieties made—smooth, crepey, soft, stiff, elastic, polished. Sheers and tricots sometimes have satin faces.

**satin finish**   Glossy finish given to many fabrics; a broad term in the trade.

**saxony**   General term for finest quality woolens made of short-staple, botany wools of superior felting power. May be stock dyed, piece dyed, or yarn dyed. Sometimes used to designate a particular type of fabric, such as saxony coating, saxony flannel, etc. Also, a fine knitting yarn.

**Sayelle** Trademark owned by Du Pont for woven or knit garments made of bicomponent Orlon acrylic fiber, types 21 or 24.

**schiffli** A machine for embroidering and making heavy venise lace. A pantagraph attachment traces the design, which is mechanically reproduced upon the fabric.

**schreinering** Embossing of 125 to 500 fine lines per inch on fabric surfaces, giving a silk-like luster. The lines produce a very large number of tiny reflecting surfaces in several planes, creating the luster.

**Scotchgard** Trademark owned by Minnesota Mining & Manufacturing Co. for a fluoride-based, stain-repellent, rain-repellent finish. Special formulations are made for leather.

**Scottish district checks** Authentic checks in true colors of particular Scottish districts designed in a wide variety of small patterns. Names of authentic district checks are: Prince of Wales, Seaforth, Glen Urquhart, Ing, Dupplin, Scots Guard, Kinlockewe, Mar, Gairloch, Fannich, Lochmore, Erchless, Invercauld, Ballindalloch, Glen Moriston, Brooke, Benmore, Coigach, Dacre, Small Glen Urquhart, Russell Guisachan, Horse Guards, Glenfeshie, Shepard Check, Strathspey.

**scottish plaid or tartan** Coarse, very durable twilled woolen fabric, made of native wool in Scotland in various tartan patterns of Scottish clans. (See clan plaid.)

**scottish tweed** Cloth with a white warp and stock-dyed filling, or vice versa. Yarns are irregular and colors often vivid, with much contrast.

**screen prints** Similar to stencil work, except that a screen of fine silk, nylon, polyester, or metal mesh is employed. Certain areas of the screen are treated to take dye, others to resist dye. A paste color is forced through the screen onto the fabric by a squeegee to form the pattern. Separate screens are used for each color in the pattern. More expensive than roller printing, but, for limited yardage and more delicate designs, often more economical.

**Sculptured**  Trademark owned by Tennessee Eastman for intermittently bulked acetate yarn similar to Loftura. Has shorter slubs.

**sea island cotton**  Valuable species of West Indies cotton having world's longest staple, sometimes 2 1/4 inches, commonly about 1 1/2 inches. Creamy white, silky seeds have very little fuzz. Used in top quality shirtings and other luxury fabrics.

**seersucker**  Lightweight cotton fabric with crinkled stripes made by weaving some warp threads slack, others tight. Woven seersucker is more expensive than chemically achieved plissés that look like seersucker.

**selvage**  Heavy reinforced outside woven edges of cloth. Sometimes spelled "selvedge."

**sequin**  Small metal or plastic plate or disc used as trimming. Also called *spangle* and *paillette*. (See paillette.)

**Serene**  Trademark owned by Fiber Industries for polyester tow for quilting, pillows.

**serge**  Twill weave with the diagonal prominent on both sides of the cloth.

**sericulture**  Raising of silkworms to produce raw silk.

**serpentine crepe**  Plain weave with lengthwise crinkled effect. Also in ribbed form with heavy filling in the ribs.

**set**  A set yarn is one that has been textured, then subjected to heat prior to removing the texture.

**105**

**shadow lace**   Very lightweight machine-made laces with mesh ground and shadow-like patterns in closer mesh.

**shag**   1. Originally a stout haircloth made of coarse wool in the Orkney Islands. 2. Coarse, long-napped woolen coatings. 3. Mixture of wool and flax used in England before cotton was available for mixtures; red shag blankets were sent to America for trading purposes with the Indians before 1620.

**Shag-o-lon**   Trademark owned by Glenn of America, yarn spinner, for Turbo-processed acrylic yarns. Also uses mark *Shag-Paca* for Turbo-processed acrylic.

**shantung**   Plain silk weave originally made in Shantung Province of China, on hand looms from wild silk. Characterized by rough, nubbed surface caused by knots and slubs in the yarn.

**Shareen**   Trademark owned by Courtaulds for producer-textured nylon yarn for hosiery.

**sharkskin**   Hard-finished simple twill or basket-weave worsted suiting of one color crossed with white. Also plain sports weave of dull luster acetate or triacetate.

**Shebonized**   Trademark owned by Sheble, yarn processor, for Turbo-processed acrylic yarn.

**sheer**   Any very thin fabric such as organdy, voile, chiffon, net, etc. The terms *heavy sheer* and *semi-sheer* describe more dense fabrics made from the fine yarns used in sheers.

**shetland**   1. Name should apply only to wool from sheep raised in the Shetland Isles of Scotland. Fabrics made of it are extremely lightweight and warm, with a raised finish and soft hand. 2. A type of knitting yarn.

**shoddy**   Re-manufactured wool fibers obtained by garnetting, or shredding, discarded woolen, worsted, or knitted garments.

Often mixed or blended with better quality and long-staple fibers to make inexpensive fabrics.

**shrinkage** Treatments to remove most of a fabric's tendency to shrink. Sponging, steaming, machine shrinking, cold-water shrinking, and resin applications are some of the more common techniques.

**Signette** Trademark owned by Association Spinners for spun-dyed acrylic yarn.

**silk** An animal fiber composed of two filaments (brins) encased in gum reeled from the cocoon of the silkworm, either cultivated or wild.

**silk weighting** Process used in silk dyeing to add weight, generally employing tin salts (stannic chloride), but tannin may be used for blacks. Federal Trade Commission requires weighted silks to be so specified.

**Silspun** Trademark owned by Dixie Yarns, processor, for spun yarns of man-made fibers.

**sisal** A hard fiber obtained from the swordlike leaves of the sisal plant, *Agava sisalana*.

**Skapalon** Trademark owned by Kayser-Roth for nylon stretch hosiery yarn used by firm's Schiaparelli Division.

**skein-dyed yarns** Either spun or filament yarns of any natural or man-made fiber dyed in the form of hanks or skeins.

**Skenandoa rayon** Trademark owned by Skenandoa Rayon Corp. (subsidiary of Beaunit Corp.) for viscose rayon fiber. Other mark: *Skendo,* for viscose filament yarn.

**skip-dent** "Skip" in a weave producing "holes" in a fabric, usually massed in a patterned effect such as stripes.

**Skybloom**  Trademark owned by American Enka Corp. for high-crimp staple rayon tufting yarn.

**Skyloft**  Trademark owned by American Enka Corp. for bulked filament viscose rayon yarn.

**slashing**  The treatment of threads or yarns with starch, gelatin, and other compounds to prevent them from breaking during the weaving process.

**slippage**  Sliding or slipping of warp threads along filling threads, or vice versa, in a fabric of smooth yarns or loose weave. Sometimes useful in fabrics where bias stretch is wanted.

**slipper satin**  Strong, compact satin of silk, rayon, acetate, synthetics, or mixtures of fibers. Sometimes with cotton back.

**slub**  Soft, thick, uneven nub in a yarn that gives decorative textured effect to a weave.

**SM-27**  Trademark owned by Courtaulds North America Inc. for high-wet-strength viscose rayon staple. Formerly called *Moynel,* now called *Lirelle.*

**Sno-Mat**  Trademark owned by Dillon-Beck, molder, for interlocking olefin plastic links used for artificial ski slopes. Made from Celanese Fortiflex polyethylene.

**snow cloth**  Fabric knitted or woven, then heavily fulled or felted. Often treated to be water repellent.

**Softglo**  Trademark owned by American Enka Corp. for semi-dull filament viscose rayon yarns mainly for upholstery fabrics.

**Soft-Loft**  Trademark owned by Grove, yarn processor, for bulky yarn.

**108**

**Softyon**   Trademark owned by Northern Yarn, yarn processor, for textured yarns made via the firm's own process.

**solution dyeing**   Rayon or man-made fiber fabrics sometimes are dyed by adding color to the chemical polymer before fibers are formed. Colors are fast and durable. Also called *dope dyeing.*

**Sontique**   Trademark owned by Du Pont as certification mark for sleep products made of Dacron Type 108 fiberfill.

**Source**   Trademark owned by Allied Chemical for biconstituent fiber made of nylon 6 filaments with embedded polyester fibrils running parallel to axis of filament. The only such biconstituent fiber on the market.

**soutache**   Narrow decorative trouser braid used chiefly for sewing ornamental designs on garments.

**Spandelle**   Trademark owned by Firestone Synthetic Fibers Co. for a fused multifilament spandex elastomer. Called "Spanzelle" in England. (Production discontinued in April, 1966.)

**spandex***   Generic name established by Federal Trade Commission for "a manufactured fiber in which the fiber-forming substance is a long-chain synthetic polymer comprised of at least 85% of a segmented polyurethane." These are the common elastomers of stretch fibers.

**spanish lace**   Any lace made in Spain. The most common is silk with heavy flat floral designs held together with varying meshes.

**sparkling nylon**   Trademark owned by Du Pont for a trilobal cross-section 15-denier nylon monofilament.

* *ed. note:* The term "spandex" is not a generic term abroad. Mass use of it outside the United States might conflict with the rights of third parties in similar names or trademarks.

**109**

**Spark-L-ite**   Trademark owned by Enjay Fibers for high-luster saran monofilaments for outdoor furniture webbing.

**Spectrell**   Trademark owned by Deering Milliken for a skein-dyed Orlon acrylic yarn.

**Spectrodye**   Trademark owned by American Enka Corp. for producer-sequentially-dyed nylon textured filament yarn for carpet. Multilobal profile.

**Spinlon**   Trademark owned by Spinlon, yarn processor, for textured nylon, olefin, or polyester yarns.

**spinneret**   A metallic cap or jet with microscopic holes in the surface through which spinning solutions are forced, emerging as fine filaments into a coagulating medium such as water, air, etc.

**Springset**   Trademark owned by U.S. Rubber Co. for textured spun-nylon carpet yarn.

**spunbonded**   Term coined by Du Pont to describe sheet structures formed from continuous filaments in a process integrating fiber spinning, web forming, and bonding.

**Spuncora**   Trademark owned by Textured Yarn, processor, for its textured yarns.

**Spunized**   Trademark owned by Spunize Co. of America for crimped textured non-torque filament yarns.

**Spun-Lo**   Trademark owned by Spun-Lo Eiderlon Inc. for knit acetate fabrics.

**spun silk**   Yarn made of silk broken by emergence of mature silk moths from cocoons.

**stabilizing**  Any process which prevents fabrics from both shrinking or stretching.

**stain-and-spot resistance**  Resins and silicone and fluoride finishes when applied to fabric give cloth the ability to resist water- and oil-borne staining.

**stannic chloride**  Tin salts used in weighting silk.

**staple**  Several textile meanings: 1. Fiber in its raw state. 2. Length of the raw fiber, both natural and man-made. Usually short lengths rather than one continuous strand or filament. 3. Basic item of merchandise regularly produced and sold.

**Star**  Trademark owned by Hystron for star-shaped pentalobal-profile polyester. (See Trevira.)

**Star Breeze**  Trademark owned by Beaunit Fibers for a cuprammonium rayon filament yarn.

**Star Spun**  Trademark owned by American Thread for Turbo-processed high-bulk acrylic knitting yarns.

**Stevetex**  Trademark owned by J. P. Stevens for a patented process for texturizing multiple ends of warp yarns at the same time while on a warp beam.

**stock dyeing**  Fiber dyed in raw state before being spun into yarn.

**storm serge**  In the U.S., seven-ounce twill; harsh, wiry, and lustrous; lower quality than regular serge.

**Stranglas**  Trademark owned by Fiberfil for glass filament yarn.

**Strata-Slub**  Trademark owned by Beaunit Fibers for thick-and-thin cuprammonium rayon continuous filament yarn.

**Stratella**    Trademark owned by Beaunit Fibers for a rayon filament yarn with naps.

**Strawn**    Trademark owned by Midland-Ross for a flat straw-like rayon yarn for draperies and upholstery.

**Stretch-Ever**    Trademark owned by International Latex Corp. for elastic fabrics made of spandex and sold in foundation garments made by Sarong, Inc., a subsidiary.

**stretch fabrics**    These are cloths with yield and return properties built in. There are three basic types: 1. Fabrics incorporating rubber yarns or threads. 2. Fabrics utilizing stretch nylon or polyester yarns. 3. Types made from core-spun spandex yarns or bare or covered spandex. (Note: it is also possible to give a cloth stretch properties through chemical or mechanical treatments.)

**Stretchon**    Trademark owned by Southern Silk Mills for stretch and bulked yarns.

**Stretchspun**    Trademark owned by Associated Spinners, yarn processors, for textured spun yarns of acrylic, polyester, wool, and other fibers.

**strié**    Irregular streaks in a fabric of practically the same color as the background.

**stripe**    Pattern formed by lengthwise or crosswise lines of narrow bands of a different color, structure, material, weave, etc.

**Strongspun**    Trademark owned by American Viscose Division of FMC for strong staple rayon.

**Sublistatic**    A method of fabric printing using a decal process that transfers the design from paper to fabric via heat and rollers. Most often used in printing on circular knits.

**suede cloth**   Woven or knitted fabric with surface finished to resemble suede leather.

**Sunspun**   Trademark owned by Beaunit Fibers for a rayon filament yarn.

**Super-Cordura**   Trademark owned by Du Pont for high-tenacity rayon yarn.

**Super-L**   Trademark owned by FMC for smooth soil-resistant rayon carpet fiber.

**Superloft**   Trademark owned by Leesona Corp. for false-twist filament textured stretch bulk or torque thermoplastic fibers twisted in a heated zone.

**Super-Narco**   Trademark owned by Beaunit Fibers for super-high-tenacity viscose rayon filament.

**Super-Rayflex**   Trademark owned by American Viscose Division of FMC for high-strength continuous filament rayon yarn 40% stronger than regular Rayflex.

**Superset**   Trademark owned by American Cyanamid for a durable wrinkle-resistant finish.

**Supima**   Trademark adopted by the Supima Association of America for extra-long-staple cotton fiber grown in American Southwest. Minimum length of fibers is 1 3/8; 1 7/16 is average; some are as long as 1 1/2 inches.

**Suprenka**   Trademark owned by American Enka Corp. for high-tenacity rayon filament yarn.

**surah**   Soft, lustrous silk in serge or twill weave. Often in other fibers.

**swatch** Small piece of cloth used as a sample of a fabric.

**Swimstretch** Trademark owned by Burlington Industries for nylon filament yarn textured via ARCT or Superloft system.

**synthetic fibers** Growing list of manufactured fibers that result from chemical syntheses. Differ from rayon in that rayon fiber is based on regenerating cellulose or acetate, which is a regenerated ester of cellulose.

# T

**T-45** Trademark owned by Beaunit Fibers for bright and black rayon tow with 12% shrinkage for direct spinning.

**taffeta** Basic plain weave with warp and filling approximately of the same count. Smooth on both sides, usually with a sheen. May be plain, printed, striped, checked, plaided, or antique with uneven threads. Made in various weights, from heavy to paper thin.

**taffetized finish** Crisp finish, often non-permanent, applied to give taffeta-like appearance and rustle.

**tapa cloth** Fabric pounded out in flat unwoven webs by natives of Pacific Islands from the bast or bark of the paper mulberry tree. May be as fine as muslin or tough and leathery; can be bleached, dyed, and printed. Also called *bark cloth*.

**tapestry** Originally Oriental embroideries worked with colored worsted, gold, or silver threads; now widely imitated in dobby, jacquard, and embroidery effects. Distinctive tapestry designs are associated with such names as Verdures, Gothic, Renaissance, Arras, Lille, Brussels, Gobelin, Savonnerie, Beauvais, and Aubusson.

**tarlatan**  Stiffened thin open-mesh transparent muslin used for stiffening garments, fancy dress costumes, Christmas stockings, petticoats, etc.

**tartan**  Woolen cloth made with 2/2 twill in plaids of various colors, worn chiefly by Scottish Highlanders, each clan having its distinct pattern. (See clan plaid.)

**Tartan Turf**  Trademark owned by 3M (Minnesota Mining & Manufacturing) for crimped round-profile cut-section nylon fiber bonded to polyester backing for use as recreational surfaces.

**Taslan**  Trademark owned by Du Pont for a mechanical method of substantially changing the loft, texture, covering power, and feel of textile yarns through air bulking. (See air jet.)

**tassel**  Pendant ornament ending in a tuft of loose threads.

**Tastex**  Trademark owned by Caron, yarn spinner, for Taslan-processed acrylic yarns.

**tattersalls**  Boldly colored plaids named after London horse-market blankets.

**tatting**  Knotted lace worked with fingers and shuttle. Made in various designs, cloverleaf and wheel being the most popular.

**Tebilized**  Trademark owned by Tootal Broadhurst Lee Co., Ltd., for fabrics processed for crease resistance and licensed to those cloths that meet firm's performance standards. Applied mainly to linens, cottons, and spun rayons.

**Tech-Sured**  Trademark owned by Associated Spinners, yarn processors, for nylon, polyester, and acrylic textured yarns.

**115**

**Teflon**  Trademark owned by Du Pont for fluorocarbon filament yarn, staple, tow, and flock.

**Telron**  Trademark owned by Robertson Carpet for solution-dyed acrylic carpet yarn purchased from private source.

**Templon**  Trademark owned by Templon, yarn processor, for Turbo-processed, high-bulk Orlon stretch yarn.

**tenacity**  A measure of yarn strength. High tenacity denotes high strength.

**Tenite**  Trademark owned by Eastman for olefin ribbon yarn for tufted carpet backings and face yarns.

**Tergal**  Trademark owned by Rhodiaceta S.A. for polyester fiber produced in France.

**terry cloth**  Cotton toweling, woven or knitted, covered with loops on one or both sides. Extremely water absorbent. Types for fashion apparel are lightweight, fancies or plain. Now available in stretch versions.

**Terylene**  Trademark of Imperial Chemical Industries. Ltd. (U.K.), for filament and staple polyester fiber produced in Britain, various European countries, and Canada.

**Texlon**  Trademark owned by Texlon, yarn processor, for thermoplastic false-twist yarns.

**Tex-Set**  Trademark owned by Texlon, yarn processor, for false-twist set textured yarns for knitwear.

**Textralized**  Trademark owned by Joseph Bancroft & Sons Co. for textured yarns made by stuffer box crimping technique.

**Textura**  Trademark owned by Textured Yarn, processor, for multicolor nylon textured filament yarn.

**textured** Generic term for a variety of bulked yarns that have greater volume and surface interest than conventional yarn of same fiber and denier. These include loopy, high-bulked, or crimped types.

**Texture Engineered** Trademark owned by Duplan, yarn processor, for textured nylon and polyester yarns.

**Texturset** Trademark owned by Ames, yarn processor, for textured yarns for rugs and pile fabrics.

**Textryl** Descriptive term set by Du Pont for a new type of non-woven textile structure made from spunbonded fibrids. The trademark is registered abroad for defensive purposes only. (See Fibrid.)

**thick-and-thin yarn** Continuous filament novelty yarn made purposely uneven in the spinning operation.

**Thornel** Trademark owned by Union Carbide for continuous filament graphite yarns converted from rayon by heat.

**thread** Usually a strand of yarn that has been plied, twisted, and finished for smoothness, used in sewing.

**throwing** The doubling, twisting, tetxurizing, or modifying of filament yarns to create new aesthetic effects.

**tie silk** Any of the silk fabrics used in making men's neckwear, often foulard, plain, or printed with small patterns.

**tissue** Formerly a fine silk fabric richly colored and ornamented, usually interwoven with gold or silver threads. Now sheer fabric or gauze or, more generally, any woven fabric of fine quality.

**titer** Refers to weight per unit length of yarn. Also the number of filaments in reeled silk thread.

**117**

**toile**  1. General French term for all kinds of coarse plain-weave linen or cotton fabrics. 2. Cotton printed with fine-line pictorial design as in "toile de Jouy." 3. Cut-out unbleached muslin pattern of a garment.

**top-dyed**  Refers to wool which is dyed when in the form of a loose rope of parallel fibers made by a combing machine, prior to spinning fibers into worsted yarn to make worsted cloth.

**Topel**  Trademark owned by Courtaulds N.A. Inc. for cross-linked rayon fiber to blend with other fibers such as cotton, acetate, and nylon.

**torchon**  Bobbin lace made of coarse thread in simple, fan-like or diamond-shaped design, with little background. Similar to cluny but without "wheat-ear" or "wheel" motifs. Durable; used for trimming household linens rather than apparel.

**torque yarns**  Generic term for yarns that tend to rotate or twist when hung freely. "S" twist rotates clockwise; "Z" twist rotates counter-clockwise.

**Totarn**  Trademark owned by American Silk Mills for spun viscose rayon yarns made from tow.

**Touch**  Trademark owned by Allied Chemical for fine-denier modified-Y-profile nylon fiber with silky hand cover and appearance of textured yarns. Mainly for apparel.

**Tough Stuff**  Trademark owned by Beaunit Fibers for high-tenacity polyester fiber.

**tow**  Large number of continuous filaments drawn and collected in loose rope-like strand without definite twist, suitable for cutting into staple or flock or further processing into spun yarns.

**transparent velvet**  Rayon pile with rayon or silk back, usually crush-resistant finish. Translucent when held to light.

**Trevira**  Trademark owned by Hystron for round-profile filament and staple polyester fiber. (See Star.)

**triacetate**  Differs from regular cellulose acetate, which is a diacetate. The description implies the extent of acetylation and degree of solubility in acetone. Fiber resists more heat than acetate, generally holds pleats, shape, and texture.

**Tricocel**  Trademark owned by Celanese Fibers Co. for acetate tricot yarn.

**tricot**  French for warp-knitted fabric. Tricots are flat knitted with fine ribs on the face (lengthwise) and ribs on the back (widthwise).

**tricotine**  Weave similar to gabardine but with a steep double-twill weave with a knitted effect. Also called *cavalry twill*.

**Trinese**  Trademark owned by Celanese Mexicana S.A. for triacetate filament yarn and staple made and sold in Mexico.

**tropical suiting**  Lightweight suiting for hot-weather wear. Usually has clear finish and hard-twist yarns.

**T-1700**  Trademark owned by Tennessee Eastman for an elastic monofilament polyester fiber. Fiber is experimental only and not available at this time.

**tufted fabric**  Fabric decorated with fluffy tufts of soft-twist, multiple-ply yarns. Usually hooked by needle into fabric structure or by tufting machine at high speeds.

**Tufton**  Trademark owned by Grace for olefin monofilament fiber for carpet backing.

**tulle**  Fine, lightweight, soft, machine-made net. The small meshes are usually hexagonal. Used for bridal veils, formal gowns, etc.

**Tultrim**  Trademark owned by Imperial Chemical Industries for newly developed heterofil nylon fleece fiber. Designed initially for carpet markets, the filament fiber is said to have a normal polyamide core surrounded by an outer crust made from a monomer with a low melt point.

**Turbo**  Trademark owned by Turbo for special processing method that utilizes Turbonizing equipment to impart high-bulk properties to acrylic yarns.

**Turbo-Glo**  Trademark owned by Malina, yarn processor, for glitter high-bulk yarns combined with metallics.

**Turning Point**  Merchandising trademark owned by FMC offering six-year guarantee for carpets made of Avlin polyester.

**tussah**  1. General term for uncultivated or wild silk. 2. Specifically silk filaments from the tussah worm of India (*Attacus myllita*), or of China (*Attacus pernyi*). Worms feed on leaves of the oak tree, castor bean plant, etc. Cocoons are larger than those of domestic silkworms, which feed on mulberry leaves. Filaments are coarser, crisper, stronger, and more irregular, brownish in color.

**Tusson**  Trademark owned by Beaunit Fibers for nep rayon filament yarn.

**tweed**  Fabric of rough, unfinished appearance, soft and flexible. Usually mixed color effects. Also plain colors, checks, and plaids. Term "tweed" now loosely applied to many casual woolens and simulations in cottons, silks, blends, knits, etc.

**twill**  Weave with diagonal ribs and large number of variations. Diagonals may be set at sharp or blunt angles, may be embedded or raised. Important types are flannels, serges, gabardines, and surahs.

**Twin-Spun**  Merchandising trademark owned by Du Pont for certified knits of Orlon acrylic.

**twist**  The turning of fibers or yarns around their axes, expressed in number of turns per unit of length.

**twist-yarn cloth**  Fabric made from two or more colored yarns twisted or plied together, giving a mottled effect. Also called *marl*.

**Tyco**  Trademark owned by Textured Yarn, processor, for textured yarns.

**Tycora**  Trademark owned by Textured Yarn Co. for several processes used to modify continuous filament yarns of various types.

**Typar**  Trademark owned by Du Pont for spunbonded material made of olefin fibers, designed primarily as backing for tufted carpets and rugs.

**Typé**  Trademark owned by Bancroft for textralized bouclé-type yarn.

**Tyrex**  Collective trademark used by members of fiber industry who make high-tenacity viscose tire yarns that meet Tyrex Tire Cord specifications.

**Tyron**  Trademark owned by Midland-Ross for high-tenacity rayon filament for industrial uses.

**Tyvek**  Trademark owned by Du Pont for spunbonded high-density material made of olefin fibers and used as wall-covering substrate, for disposable apparel, or industrial uses.

**Tyweld**   Trademark owned by Midland-Ross for adhesive-treated high-tenacity yarns and cords for industrial applications mainly.


## U

**Ultrason**   Trademark owned by Ultrasona, and licensed exclusively in the U.S. to Berkshire International for a process of texturizing finished nylon hosiery by application of ultrasonic waves. Process changes the molecular structure of yarns, giving them a matte look. In the U.K., the process is called *Nysilk*.

**Ultravat**   Trademark owned by Metlon Corp. for polyester-coated metal yarn that resists light fading in outdoor and automotive uses.

**Unel**   Trademark owned by Union Carbide for a fused spandex monofilament yarn for hosiery and foundations.

**unfinished**   (1) Woolen fabrics not fulled and sheared. (2) Worsted fabrics, pressed or sheared a little but otherwise left as they come from the loom.

**Unibond**   Trademark owned by United Piece Dye Works for its process for adhesive fabric-to-fabric bonding of man-made woven fabrics.

**Unidure**   Trademark owned by United Piece Dye Works for permanent wrinkle-resistant finish for spun rayons and blends.

**Unifast**   Trademark owned by United Piece Dye Works for a finish for spun rayons to impart washability and limited shrinkage.

**Uniglass**   Trademark owned by United Merchants & Manufacturers for glass fiber fabrics. Mostly for industrial or decorative uses.

**union-dyed** Fabric made of two or more fibers dyed in one bath with each type of fiber taking a different color simultaneously. Often dyes cooperate to give a mixed-fiber cloth a single uniform shade or a novelty effect.

**Uni-Prest** Trademark owned by United Piece Dye Works for durable-press soil-release finish for rayon and polyester fabrics.

**UniROYAL** Trademark owned by UniRoyal as a worldwide trademark, replacing "U.S. Rubber" trademark.

**Unisec** Trademark owned by United Piece Dye Works for a water-repellent, crease-resistant, spot-resistant resin finish.

**United** Trademark owned by United Saran for an olefin monofilament fiber produced in Israel.

**Unitru** Trademark owned by Spinlon, yarn processor, for textured yarn.

**Uspun** Trademark owned by UniRoyal for all blends of natural and man-made fibers made into spun yarns.


# V

**Valenciennes or val** Bobbin lace. Mesh ground, with floral or scroll design, usually outlined by a line of open work. Dainty sheer effects. Popular in edging form.

**Vanilon** Trademark owned by Van Raalte for nylon yarn for one-size pantyhose.

**Variline** Trademark owned by American Enka for random-colored nylon filament yarns.

**vat-dyed**  Material that has been dyed by insoluble vat colors produced on the fabric by oxidation. Considered the most resistant to both washing and sunlight. Originally applied to fabrics in big wooden vats, hence the name.

**Vectra**  Trademark owned by Enjay Chemical for polypropylene filament and olefin staple yarns.

**Veldown**  Trademark owned by Schwarzenbach for ARCT-processed texturized nylon yarns.

**velours**  French for "velvet." Fabric raised on surface in finishing so as to have a close, dense, erect, and even nap, providing a soft hand and velvety look. Originally made of wool, now made in other fibers also.

**velvet**  Warp pile fabric with short-cut close pile that gives a smooth rich surface, soft to the touch. Effect is obtained by weaving two faces together and shearing apart. One type of "loop" velvet has an uncut pile. Pile may be chemically dissolved to leave patterns on a chiffon or taffeta ground. Also, pile may be pressed flat, as in panné velvet, or cut and uncut loops may be combined to form a pattern.

**velveteen**  Cotton or rayon pile fabric with short, close filling loops cut by sharp knives to create an erect velvety pile. Unlike velvet, which is woven face to face, velveteen is woven singly. Back may be plain weave or twill. The twill is better quality, more expensive, holds the pile more firmly.

**venise**  Point lace without net background. Designs of elaborate florals, and scrolls are thrown into relief by heavy overstitching. In machine-made venise, the design is usually embroidered ground on a fabric, removed later by chemical process leaving the embroidery only.

**124**

**venturia** Trademark owned by Leon-Ferenbach Inc. for an air-bulked novelty yarn made via the Taslan process.

**Vercelli** Trademark owned by Glen Raven for core-spun yarn of Lycra sheathed with Orlon acrylic and nylon fibers.

**Verel** Trademark owned by Eastman Chemical Products Inc. for modacrylic staple, filament, and yarn.

**Veri-Dul** Trademark owned by Beaunit Fibers for a dull viscose rayon filament yarn.

**Verve** Trademark owned by Bibb Mfg. Co. for core-spun yarns of many types.

**vicuna** Wool of the vicuna, a llama-like animal of the Andes, the finest fiber classified as wool. Expensive and scarce. Sale of the fiber is regulated by Peruvian government. Reddish-brown color, pronounced silk luster, exceptionally soft handle, makes lush, soft, luxury coatings, highest priced in the market.

**vigoureaux printed yarn** Worsted yarn printed before weaving to give a mixed-color effect in the weave.

**Villwyte** Trademark owned by Midland-Ross for rayon filament yarn for conversion into carbonized or graphitized fabrics or yarns.

**vinal** Generic term established by FTC for a "manufactured fiber in which the fiber-forming substance is any long-chain synthetic polymer composed of at least 50% by weight of vinyl alcohol units and in which the total of the vinyl alcohol units and any one or more of the acetate units is at least 85% by weight of the fiber."

**Vincel** Trademark owned by Courtaulds for high-wet-modulus rayon produced in U.K. and marketed in U.S. by Courtaulds NA.

**125**

**Vinyon** Formerly a trademark of Union Carbide Co., now an FTC generic name for fiber classification. Defined as "a manufactured fiber in which the fiber-forming substance is any long-chain synthetic polymer composed of at least 85% by weight of vinyl chloride units."

**virgin wool** According to the Wool Products Labeling Act of 1939, virgin wool, also called *new wool,* is: "wool that has never been used, or reclaimed from any spun, woven, knitted, felted, manufactured, or used product." The term is no guarantee of quality, because any grade of wool can be "virgin wool".

**viscose rayon** Manufactured fiber made of regenerated cellulose, most commonly obtained from wood pulp.

**Vision-ora** Trademark owned by Belmont, yarn processor, for nylon or polyester filament yarn.

**Vitalized** Trademark owned by U.S. Finishing Co., an American licensee, for a crush-resistant process of the Tootal Broadhurst Lee Co., England.

**Vitel** Trademark owned by Goodyear for resin used in spinning Vycron, polyester, and other man-made fibers.

**Vitro-flex** Trademark owned by Johns-Manville for glass filament yarns.

**voile** Lightweight sheer plain weave with crisp airy feel. Made from yarns having considerably more than normal twist.

**Volari** Trademark owned by National Spinning, yarn processor, for textured filament yarns.

**Vycron** Trademark owned by Beaunit Corp's Fiber Division for polyester filament, staple, and tow.

**Vylor** Trademark owned by Du Pont for nylon monofilament yarn and ribbons for industrial thread.

**Waffle cloth**  Fabric with a characteristic honeycomb weave, such as waffle piqué.

**wale**  Ridge or rib in a knitted or woven fabric. Wales may run crosswise, lengthwise, or diagonally.

**warp**  Set of lengthwise yarns in a loom through which the crosswise filling yarns (weft) are interlaced. Sometimes called *ends*.

**warp knits**  Usually tricots. Are knitted on flat-bed warp-knitting machines at high speeds up to 1,000 courses per minute. Threads run in loops in a generally lengthwise direction. They zigzag slightly to join adjacent loops. Warp knitting can produce a variety of fabrics in a variety of effects including stripes, checks, plaids, mesh fabrics, nets, and laces. Plain tricots are familiar in lingerie.

**warp prints**  Blurred designs achieved in woven fabrics by printing the warp threads before fabrics are woven. Subsequent weaving gives the soft blurred effect.

**wash-and-wear**  Fabrics or garments which require little or no touch-up ironing after washing. Term has been eclipsed by relatively new development of durable press, which some describe as the true wash-and-wear. (See durable press.)

**washable**  Fabrics which will not fade or shrink when washed according to specified directions.

**waterproofing**  Fabrics are made completely waterproof by treatment with coatings of rubber, resin, or plastic. "Waterproof" and "water-repellent" do not have exact meanings, but "waterproof" is the more absolute.

**water-repellent**  Many trademarked water-repellent finishes are used to make fabrics resist water absorption. They include chemical, resin, silicone, and fluoride types designed to make cloth more resistant to water, spots, and stains. Such terms as "shower-proof," "water-retarding," "water-resistant" are also used to describe them.

**Wear Dated**   Merchandising trademark owned by Monsanto for one-year guarantee for finished garments.

**Weatherbright**   Trademark owned by Dow Badische for a carpet-yarn blend of Zefkrome acrylic and Kanekalon modacrylic fibers.

**weaving**   The process of manufacturing fabric by interlacing a series of warp yarns with filling yarns at right angles.

**Welderstretch**   Trademark owned by Blackwelder, yarn processor, for nylon stretch yarn.

**Wellene**   Trademark owned by Wellman for polyester filament yarn in trilobal profile.

**Wellon**   Trademark owned by Wellman for nylon 66 fiber.

**Wellstrand**   Trademark owned by Wellman for nylon and polyester heavy-denier fiber for athletic fields and golf courses.

**whipcord**   Usually bold upright warp twill, with about a 63-degree angle and a clear finish that emphasizes the diagonal cord or twill. Used for riding habits, service uniforms, etc.

**wild silk**   Silk produced by a great variety of silkworms feeding on other than mulberry leaves. Tussah is a wild silk.

**Wintuk**   Certification mark owned by Du Pont for yarns and fabrics made of monocomponent and bicomponent staple of Orlon acrylic.

**Wither-White**   Trademark owned by Celanese Corp. of America for viscose filament rayon yarn.

**Woodtone Mylar**   Trademark owned by Metlon Corp. for polyester slit yarn in subtle blond wood color simulating bamboo strips, used in wood weaves.

**wool**   The fleece of sheep. Chemically a member of the class of keratin proteins.

**woolens**   Wide range of fabrics made from woolen yarns (undercoat wool of sheep), varying in quality, construction, and looks. Compared with worsteds, they are generally more simple weaves with fulled or raised surfaces more or less obscuring the weave. Some cloths are fulled to almost felt-like texture. Typical woolens include tweeds, coatings, meltons, etc.

**worsted**   Yarn made from the hard "tops" of raw wool. Fabrics made of worsted are closely constructed of smooth, well-twisted yarns. Minimum finishing is required; cloths are left with clear surface. Fancy weaves, stock and yarn dyes are usual. Worsteds include hard suiting fabrics, flannels, crepes, etc. Generally more expensive than woolens.

**Wrinkl-Shed**   Trademark owned by Dan River Mills Inc. for a permanent-crease, soil-, mildew-, and shrink-resistant process applied to cottons.


## X

**Xena**   Trademark owned by Beaunit Fibers for high-wet-modulus staple rayon. Also merchandising trademark for fabrics meeting certain performance standards.

**Xtra-dull**   Trademark owned by Beaunit Fibers for rayon dull filament yarn.

# Y

**yarn**  Descriptive term for an assemblage of fibers of filaments, either manufactured or natural, twisted or laid together so as to form a continuous strand which can be used in weaving or knitting, or otherwise made into a textile material.

**yarn-dyed fabrics**  Fabrics in which the yarn is dyed before weaving or knitting.

# Z

**"Z" twist**   (See torque yarns.)

**Zantrel**  Trademark owned by American Enka Corp. for polynostic rayon staple fiber.

**Zefran**  Trademark owned by Dow Badische for acrylic staple fiber.

**Zefkrome**  Trademark owned by Dow Badische for solution-dyed acrylic staple fiber.

**zein**  A protein extracted from corn, usually by treatment of corn gluten with alcohol. Used in making fibers.

**Zelan**  Trademark owned by Du Pont for a durable, water-repellent, spot-resistant finishing process.

**Zeset**  Trademark owned by Du Pont for a process producing crease-resistant and shrink-resistant effects on fabrics principally of cellulosic fibers, as well as wool.

**zibeline**  Woolen fabric made in coating and suiting weights; has long hair, "laid-down" lustrous nap running in one direction. Often camel's hair or mohair shows in the nap.

# Reference Guide to Textile Labeling

## TEXTILE FIBER PRODUCTS IDENTIFICATION ACT

PART THREE

## Framework for Industry Labeling

Generic terms for man-made fibers were promulgated in 1960 by the U.S. Federal Trade Commission under authority of the Textile Fiber Products Identification Act. Definitions were established according to chemical composition of the fiber-forming substances rather than fiber properties or producer designations. The terms serve as a framework for the industry's labeling, advertising, and promotion procedures—and as protection for the consumer's interest.

Here is a ready guide for reference, updated as of November 1970.

**acetate**  A manufactured fiber in which the fiber-forming substance is cellulose acetate. Where not less than 92% of the hydroxyl groups are acetylated, the term "triacetate" may be used as a generic description of the fiber.

**acrylic**  A manufactured fiber in which the fiber-forming substance is any long-chain synthetic polymer composed of at least 85% by weight of acrylonitrile units.

**anidex**  A manufactured fiber in which the fiber-forming substance is any long-chain synthetic polymer composed of at least 50% by weight of one or more esters of a monohydric

**133**

alcohol and acrylic acid, $CH_2 = CH - COOH$ (first commercial production in U.S. was 1969, Rohm and Haas).

**azlon**  A manufactured fiber in which the fiber-forming substance is composed of any regenerated naturally occurring proteins, such as casein (skimmed milk), peanuts, and corn. (Production discontinued in U.S.)

**glass**  A manufactured fiber in which the fiber-forming substance is glass.

**lastrile**  Lastrile fibers have never been commercially produced. (See rubber.)

**metallic**  A manufactured fiber composed of metal, plastic-coated metal, metal-coated plastic, or a core completely covered by metal.

**modacrylic**  A manufactured fiber in which the fiber-forming substance is any long-chain synthetic polymer composed of less than 85% but at least 35% by weight of acrylonitrile units.

**nylon**  A manufactured fiber in which the fiber-forming substance is any long-chain synthetic polyamide having recurring amide groups as an integral part of the polymer chain.

**nytril**  A manufactured fiber containing at least 85% of a long-chain polymer of vinylidene dinitrile where the vinylidene dinitrile content is no less than every other unit in the polymer chain.

**olefin**  A manufactured fiber in which the fiber-forming substance is any long-chain synthetic polymer composed of at least 85% by weight of ethylene, propylene, or other olefin units.

**polyester**  A manufactured fiber in which the fiber-forming substance is any long-chain synthetic polymer composed of at least 85% by weight of an ester of a dihydric alcohol and terephthalic acid.

**rayon**  A manufactured fiber composed of regenerated cellulose, as well as manufactured fibers composed of regenerated cellulose in which substitutes have replaced not more than 15% of the hydrogens of the hydroxyl groups.

**rubber**  This classification recently revised by the Federal Trade Commission and expanded as follows: "A fiber in which the fiber-forming substance is composed of natural or synthetic rubber including the following categories.

"(1) a fiber in which the fiber-forming substance is a hydrocarbon such as natural rubber, polyisoprene, polybutadiene, copolymers of dienes and hydrocarbons or amorphous (noncrystalline) polyolefins.

"(2) a fiber in which the fiber-forming substance is a copolymer or acrylonitrile and a diene (such as butadiene) composed of not more than 50% but at least 10% by weight of acrylonitrile units. The term 'lastrile' may be used as a generic description for fibers falling into this category.

"(3) a fiber in which the fiber-forming substance is a polychloroprene or a copolymer of chloroprene in which at least 35% by weight of fiber-forming substance is composed of chloroprene units."

**saran**  A manufactured fiber in which the fiber-forming substance is any long-chain synthetic polymer composed of at least 80% by weight of vinylidene chloride units.

**spandex**  A manufactured fiber in which the fiber-forming substance is a long-chain synthetic polymer comprised of at least 85% of a segmented polyurethane.

**vinal**  A manufactured fiber in which the fiber-forming substance is any long-chain synthetic polymer composed of at least 50% by weight of vinyl alcohol units, and in which the total of the vinyl alcohol units and any one or more of the various acetal units is at least 85% by weight of the fiber. (No current U.S. production.)

**135**

**vinyon** A manufactured fiber in which the fiber-forming substance is any long-chain synthetic polymer composed of at least 85% by weight of vinyl chloride units.

## Characteristics of Fiber for Ready Reference

**acetate** Soft, light, strong, easy to texture, drapeable, takes colors well (triacetate similar).

**acrylic** Soft, light, fluffy, warm, quick drying, and resistant to sunlight, weather, oil, and chemicals.

**anidex** Good elastic and recovery properties.

**azlon** Soft, weak wet strength, and subject to mildew damage. No current production in U.S.

**glass** Glass fibers are actually shafts of glass. They have high strength and good resistance to heat, flame, and most chemicals. Not currently being used in apparel.

**lastrile** Lastrile fibers have never been commercially produced. Properties similar to rubber yarns.

**metallic** Coated metallic filaments will not tarnish and are generally not affected by salt water or climate.

**modacrylic** Easy to dye, flame resistant, quick drying, shape retentive, able to be softened at low temperatures, resistant to acids and alkalies. Make good wig fibers.

**nylon** Exceptionally strong, elastic when textured, abrasion resistant, lustrous, easy to wash, highly resistant to damage from oils and chemicals, low moisture absorbency, smooth, resilient, long lasting.

**nytril** Fibers are soft and resilient, soften like modacrylics at somewhat lower temperatures. Production now discontinued in U.S.

**136**

**olefin** Very light in weight, good bulk and cover, quick drying, highly stain resistant, and weather resistant. But very sensitive to heat, has somewhat waxy hand, extremely difficult to piece-dye.

**polyester** Very strong, resistant to shrinking and stretching, quick drying, crisp and resilient wet or dry, wrinkle and abrasion resistant, washable, easy to texture, retains heat-set pleats, creases, yarn distortions, and twisting.

**rayon** Absorbent, easy to dye, soft and comfortable, versatile.

**rubber** Highly elastic with good stretch properties. Used bare or in core-spun versions with wrappings or other fibers.

**saran** Strong wearing and highly resistant to sunlight, staining, fading, mildew, and weathering. Fabrics of saran can be washed with soap and water. No current apparel applications. Used mainly in industrial applications or home furnishings.

**spandex** Light in weight, excellent stretch and recovery, soft and smooth, resistant to body oils, stronger and more durable than rubber, very supple, but will degrade from exposure to ultraviolet light. Used bare or in core-spun yarns, lends lightweight freedom of movement to apparel and stretch clothing.

**vinal** Highly resistant to chemicals but softens readily at low temperature. Commonly used in industrial applications or as bonding agents for non-wovens. In some countries other than the U.S., vinyon fibers are referred to as "polyvinyl chloride fibers" or "PVC."

# How Fibers Are Made

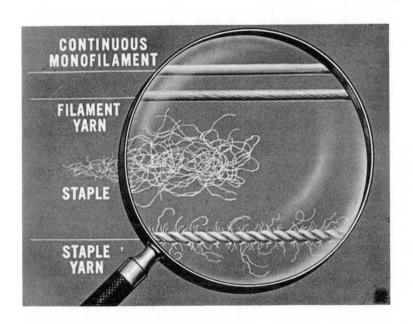

## PART FOUR

Forms of Man-Made Fibers

Courtesy of Man-Made Fibers Producers Association

**WET SPINNING**

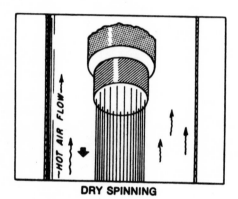

**DRY SPINNING**

**MELT SPINNING**

How Fibers Are Spun

Courtesy of Man-Made Fibers Producers Association

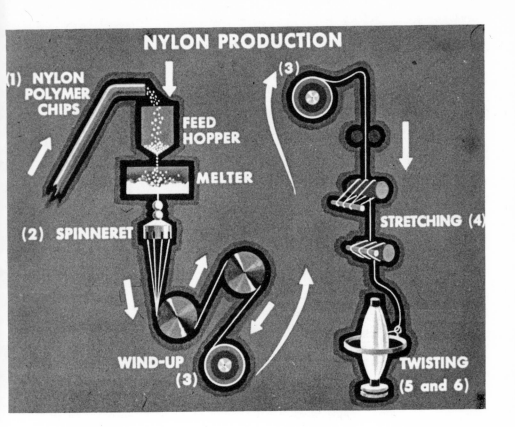

**NYLON PRODUCTION**

(1) NYLON POLYMER CHIPS

FEED HOPPER

MELTER

(2) SPINNERET

(3)

STRETCHING (4)

WIND-UP (3)

TWISTING (5 and 6)

How Nylon is Made:

1. The production of nylon fibers begins with hard white fragments called nylon polymer chips.
2. The chips are melted and the fluid is pumped to a spinneret, where it is extruded and solidified to form continuous monofilaments.
3. The assembled continuous monofilaments are taken up on a bobbin.
4. The bobbin is transported to another area where the nylon is stretched. Stretching allows the molecules within the continuous monofilaments to be arranged in a more orderly pattern.
5. The assembled continuous monofilaments are twisted into yarn.
6. The yarn is then wound onto bobbins and is ready for shipment.

Courtesy of Man-Made Fibers Producers Association

**143**

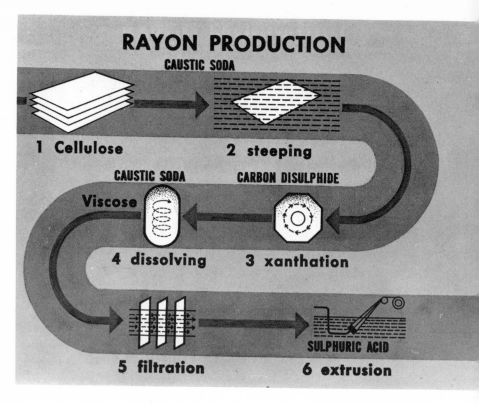

# RAYON PRODUCTION

**CAUSTIC SODA**

**1 Cellulose**

**2 steeping**

**CAUSTIC SODA**

**CARBON DISULPHIDE**

**Viscose**

**4 dissolving**

**3 xanthation**

**5 filtration**

**SULPHURIC ACID**

**6 extrusion**

How Rayon Is Made

1. Viscose rayon production begins with cellulosic sheets.
2. The sheets are steeped in caustic soda.
3. After a given period of time, the excess caustic soda solution is pressed out and the sheets are shredded into fine crumbs. After the crumbs have aged, they are chuted to tumbling barrels where carbon disulphide is added and a chemical reaction takes place. This is called the xanthation ("zanthation") process.
4. The crumbs are then fed into viscose dissolvers where they are mixed with weak caustic soda and stirred to form a viscose solution.
5. The viscose solution is filtered.
6. It is then pumped to a spinneret for extrusion into a sulphuric acid bath.

Courtesy of Man-Made Fibers Producers Association

# How Textiles Are Made

## PART FIVE

## The Textile Art

A textile is a woven fabric made by interlacing yarns. The name comes from the latin verb *texere*—which means to weave. In the broadest sense textiles include knitted fabrics, nets, laces, even non-wovens, and may be defined best as "any stuff made on a loom, knitting, or needling machine."

Historically textile structures date back as far as the Stone Age. Some of the earliest examples of textiles are linen cloths found in burial tombs of ancient Egypt used as mummy wrappings. Egyptians were weaving high-count fabrics some 4,000 years before Christ.

Greek and Roman cultures highly prized skillfully woven textiles. According to Greek legend a maiden named Arachne wove such beautiful fabrics that she challenged the Goddess Athena to equal her skill. The challenge angered Athena and she turned the boastful Arachne into a spider and condemned her to spin forever.

In the Middle Ages and the Renaissance, most weaving was done at home, and the art flourished throughout all of Europe. It took the invention of the spinning jenny and power loom in the late 1700's to free textile-making from the home and move it into the factory.

In the U.S., early American colonists—not yet wired for television—spent quiet evening hours working spinning wheels and hand looms. The first textile mill—Old Slater Mill—was built in Rhode Island in the early 1800's.

Today cloth manufacturing is a highly skilled art. It embraces straightening raw fibers, twisting them, forming them into yarns, weaving them into cloth, and dyeing and finishing.

The American Textile Manufacturers Institute estimates that United States textile mills turn out cloth at the rate of 16 miles per minute day and night for the whopping total of more than 15 billion square yards each year. That's enough to provide a strip of cloth a yard wide each day to encircle the earth at the equator—enough for 18 round trips to the moon and back each year.

The pictures spotlight the textile-making science as it stands today.—A tour through an average mill:

**Opening**   Cotton starts its trip through the mill in the opening room. Bales are opened and the fiber blended. It moves via air tubes for rapid handling.

**Carding**   Fibers are aligned, cleaned, and formed into rope-like strands called sliver, by large carding machines.

**Roving**  Here strands of sliver are combined and stretched to form new sliver in the roving frame. Strands are stretched, reduced in size, then twisted to give them strength.

**Spinning**  Fast-moving highly automated giant spinning frames stretch rovings into thin yarns and twist them further for more strength.

**Warping**  Yarns are wound on large drums called warp beams and dipped into boiling starch to give them a protective coating. This prevents breaking during weaving.

**Weaving** The giant weave shed which houses its battery of high-speed looms is the heart of the big mill. The flashing shuttles and jumping harnesses on the looms supply the magic that turns yarns into fabrics.

**Dyeing** Textiles can be dyed in the piece after weaving, colored in the yarn, or in the fiber state. Here spun yarns are being dyed in giant kettles.

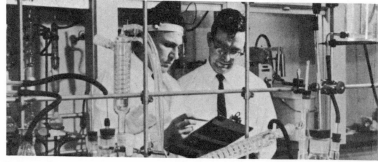

**Research** American technology means quality as well as quantity. Technicians play a vital role in developing new processes and better yarns, improving dyes and finishes, and maintaining production-line quality at highest levels.

**150**

# Major Natural Fibers and Their Sources

PART SIX

**Alpaca** Hair from a South American camaloid ruminant derived from the guanaco (*Lama huanocos*), smaller than a llama. Fiber is elastic, soft, lustrous and strong. Classified generically as wool.

**Camel Hair** Soft brilliant hair of the *Camelus* family of large ruminants. Classified Camelidea, native to desert regions of Asia and Africa. Dromedary or Arabian camel (*Camelus dromedarius*) has one hump, Bactrian camel has two. Classified generically as wool.

**Cashmere** Downy glossy undercoat hair of a small goat native to Kashmir, India. There are several species of large old world goats, family name of Ibex. Largest, *Ibex c. sibirica*, lives in Central Asia in Altai and Himalaya mountain ranges. Classified generically as wool.

**153**

**Cotton** Natural vegetable fiber produced and obtained from the boll of the Gossypium plant. Fibers range in length from 1/2 to 2 1/2 inches —the longer the better. American upland cotton, *G. hirsutum,* is a multi-branched shrub two to six feet tall which grows as an annual. Cotton's origin has been traced back to India at least to 3,000 B.C., and probably extends to many centuries earlier.

**Flax** Fibers of the flax plant of the genus *Linum.* Most important species is *Linum usitatissimum.* Crepitans variety is source of finest, whitest fibers. Use of flax dates back 10,000 years to the Stone Age. Fabrics and yarns of this fiber are called linen.

**Mohair** Long fine silky hair of the Angora goat of the species *Capra hircus,* descendant of the bezoar goat or pasang goat. Long straight mohair fibers range in length from four to 12 inches long. They are silky and lightweight, and tend to fluff up fabrics. Classified generically as wool.

**154**

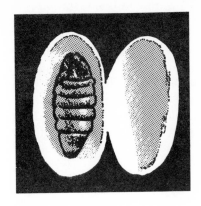

**Silk** Fine, lustrous filaments reeled from cocoons of silkworms. Each silk moth lays about 400 to 500 eggs from which small black caterpillars called "kego" (hairy babies) hatch. In about four weeks they reach adult size of several inches. The adult worm then spins a cocoon and turns into a chrysalis or pupa. In about ten days, the moth emerges—and the cycle is complete. Each single cocoon contains a continuous silk filament which may be as long as 1,300 yards.

**Vicuna** Wool from the vicuna, a slender, small ruminant mammal, *Lama vicuna*, belonging to the camel family and native to the Andes mountains in Ecuador, Peru, and Bolivia. A close relative of the domesticated llama, it has soft orange-red fur. Expensive and scarce, sale of the fiber is regulated by the Peruvian government. It's the finest fiber classified as wool, and probably the highest priced.

Some time ago, Argentine Governor Guzman of Salta Province introduced a bill in the provincial Parliament to prohibit the hunting of vicunas for 25 years. He said the shooting of the animals had intensified as a result of increased demand for vicuna wool, creating a danger that the vicuna might become extinct. Fairchild News Service estimates some 500 to 1,000 wild vicunas are slaughtered each year in Argentina for their hides. In addition, there are some two or three breeding farms with 1,000 to 1,200 animals each. Hides traded in Salta currently bring about $26 each.

**Wool** Soft, curly hair of sheep known as the fleece. Average weight of fleece from one shearing is about seven to eight pounds. Wool staple varies in length from about 1/2 inch to 18 inches. In the U.S. more than 26,000,000 sheep are raised for wool on some 340,000 farms annually. New Zealand and Australia are two other important growing nations.

# Looking at Color

## PART SEVEN

## Color . . . As I See It

Publisher's Note: When author Marvin Klapper decided to include a chapter on color in *Fabric Almanac* he turned to textile colorist José Martín. Mr. Martín, in addition to his achievements as a color expert, is an international authority on big-game fishing and nature photography. He graciously offered to write the chapter and make available illustrations from his private collection of 10,000 nature slides.

When Lew Wallace wrote "The Prince of India" late in the 19th century, little did he realize the power of his quotation: "Beauty is altogether in the eye of the beholder."

Paraphrasing it, I say color is totally within the appraisal of the viewer or the palette of the artist. While this is true, to simplify matters I prefer to think in terms of personal bias or emotional expression. Subjectively, my eyes and mind are the absolute judge, the arbiter.

When I examine the work of expressionist painters, I am convinced their perceptive powers endowed them with a certain degree of subtle discrimination of color which is not readily available to the layman.

Toulouse-Lautrec is a good example. Working with pastels as he often did, his favorite surface was pressed board, where skin tones were invariably translated into purplish blues and mustard greens. He obviously saw a vastly different range of colors than other painters under the same light conditions. He interpreted the subject matter as he saw it, in a different way from his contemporaries.

**159**

As a fabric designer and colorist I am mystified now and then by what others see in a flower . . . an insect . . . a landscape. What to me appears to be pink with purple overtones is often violet to someone else. It is this fine line of color interpretation that has sparked my curiosity to find out more, with the eye of the camera as a partner. The camera's eye is its all-seeing lens . . . its mind the receptive and obedient film. There is no subtle nuance of man's thought that can distort the picture. It's all there as nature intends.

Color as nature intends is pure color . . . the golden fleece of the artist or fashion creator.

There are those who believe color does not exist without sunlight. This is of course, altogether wrong, for it is always there, however dormant, even if not seen by the receptive eye. But what makes color come to life is light. Whether direct or bounced, light is the catalyst whose soft caress makes color live.

Whether it's in the form of the pale morning rays of a summer day in a fishing village in Nova Scotia or a breathtaking sunrise in the Bahamas, light is the means that allows us to experience the miracle of color on this planet.

You have only to stand, as I have stood, watching the sun slice the horizon and slowly vanish into the Gulf of Mexico . . . watch birds fly . . . flowers unfold . . . even tree bark grow in microscopic fractions of time . . . and you seem to hold the secret of life. Landscape is constantly changing . . . clouds drift and form patterns never duplicated through eons of time.

No matter where you turn, or how you look at things, as long as there is light, color will surround you. Even on the moon, celestial color was there to amaze and mystify our astronauts with eerie bronze greens and lunar tones, tempting earthly eyes with their beauty.

Color is everywhere to challenge and inspire artists . . . in a swamp in Georgia . . . in the blurred silhouette of an old lighthouse against the silvery gray of a September moon . . . in the red of a wild duck's beak. It's there to be captured, unaware of the telephoto lens of my camera.

The hibiscus of sharp vermilion in my garden in Florida and the thunderhead over Key Biscayne, with its pewter gray split by violent lightning into a color rhapsody, share the same intensity of excitement, due to their inimitable colors.

In this print, the soft quality of early morning fog is reminiscent of a Japanese watercolor; it is a challenge for the colorist and dyer to capture on cloth.

For more than 3,000 years man has been dyeing textiles red, scarlet, and indigo using fruits, flowers, barks, and insects. Today synthetic dyes replace Mother Nature's own colors, but none can match the intense brilliance of this scarlet zinnia . . . which remains a challenge to the dyeing industry. The soft lilac flower in the background supplies happy tonal counterpoint.

Chiaroscuro, the style of pictorial art that employs only light and shade, is an inspiration to textile colorists. Here by photographing it against the sunrise, foliage is translated into a classic chiaroscuro of sepia in low color saturation and low brilliance.

The sharp outlines of petals, and their simplicity of structure, have long made the American daisy *(Chrysanthemum leucanthemum)* a favorite theme of textile designers for print, pattern, and color inspiration. Now you can see why.

**(right**) The many moods of nature are not always expressed in brilliant colors. This dramatic study of gray touched with the glint of silver might just make the right color theme for an evening dress or theater coat.

**(below)** Texture is another dimension that fashion colorists must learn to use and control. And texture, like the bark of the Melaleuca tree, makes interesting studies in monochromatic values of light and color.

**(below right)** Ombré, the soft melting of color tones into one another is a favorite device of textile colorists. As with many other man-made techniques, its origin is nature. Here the Florida flame vine under strong sunlight is a study of ombré tones of gold with orange and yellow. What dye beck could match that beauty?

(above) Charlie, my pet chameleon, has a coat of
many colors . . . all green . . . a fascinating study in
monochromatic coloring from nature's textbook.
(above right) Geometrics in black and white are
dramatic fashion themes I find fascinating. De-
spite the many dyestuffs available today, I love to
work with black and white. This study of white
lilies in the Everglades, which I find dramatic and
exotic, will tell you why.
(below) Hot pink is my favorite color. I have used
it many times in my work and still find it soft, sen-
suous, and sexy. The pale pink showing through
the translucent throat of the Anhinga in this close-
up taken in a Florida rookery takes the highest
dyeing skill to duplicate on fabric.
(right) The Nova Scotia landscape is dotted with
the silvery gray paint of weather and salt water.
This shot, taken in Kelley's Cove, is a powerful
study of geometric shapes and unusual light values
. . . two basic tools of a colorist.

Meet Señor *Crustacea* (The American Lobster). His claw makes a fascinating study of geometric form and rich red hues to inspire an artist's palette. Red is the color most eyes see with greatest excitement. By comparison, blue and violet seem peaceful and subdued, green neutral, and yellow cheerful.

The young adult wood Ibis (*Guara, Alba*) nests in huge colonies in the Cypress swamps of Florida. I have spent many solitary hours there with my camera studying nature's color tricks for the whirlpool of fashion on Seventh Avenue.

The Atlantic sailfish (*Istiophorus, Americanus*) is a marine peacock in rich vibrant tones of blues, grays, and white. It takes the finest of yarns and the highest skills of today's textile chemists and dyers to capture these tones. But how do you capture those diamond flecks of light dancing through the proud sail?

At times the delicate intricacy of a pattern from life enchants me as much as color. A sand dune after a windstorm . . . a geometric motif of a lobster trap . . . a bird's feather . . . sea shells, all serve as design sources.

I have often been asked where an artist or colorist gets his inspirations. Where indeed? You have only to open your eyes and look around you.

Color is everywhere and truly in the eyes of the beholder.

# Principal U.S. Man-Made Fibers and Their Uses by Company

| Company | Fiber | Type | Uses |
|---|---|---|---|
| Allied | A.C.E. | nylon 6 | C |
| Chemical | Anso | anti-soil nylon | C |
| Corp. | Caprolan | nylon 6 | A, C |
|  | Source | biconstituent nylon/polyester | . C |
|  | Touch | modified X-section nylon 6 | A |
| | (polyester production planned for 1971) | | |
| American | Creslan | acrylic | A, C, HF |
| Cyanamid | DyLok | producer-dyed rayon filament | A, C, HF |
| Co. | Nupron | high-wet-modulus rayon | A |
|  | polyester | tire-cord filament | I |
|  | rayon | tire-cord filament | I |

KEY:

A    Apparel
C    Rugs & Carpet
HF  Home Furnishings Fabrics
I     Industrial

| Company | Fiber | Type | Uses |
|---|---|---|---|
| American Enka Corp. | Crepeset | producer-textured nylon | A |
| | Encron | polyester | A, HF |
| | Enkalite | multilobal polyester | C |
| | Enkaloft | nylon | C |
| | Enkalure | multilobal nylon | A, HF |
| | Enka Nylon | nylon 6 | A, C, HF |
| | Enka Rayon | rayon | A, HF |
| | Enkasheer | torque nylon | A |
| | Enkrome | acid-dyeable nylon | A, HF |
| | Jetspun | solution-dyed rayon | A, HF |
| | Kolorbon | solution-dyed rayon | A, HF |
| | Skybloom | high-crimp rayon | A, HF |
| | Skyloft | textured rayon | A, HF |
| | Spectrodye | sequestral-dyed nylon | C |
| | Variline | nylon | C |
| | Zantrel | high-modulus rayon | A, HF |
| American Viscose (Division of FMC) | Avisco | acetate | A, HF |
| | Avisco | rayon | A, C, HF |
| | Avicolor | solution-dyed acetate | A, C, HF |
| | Avicolor | solution-dyed rayon | A, C, HF |
| | Avicron | crimp rayon | C, HF |
| | Avlin | polyester | A, C, HF |
| | Avril | rayon | A, C, HF |
| | Avron | rayon | A, C, HF |
| | Fiber 25 | acetate | HF |
| Beaunit Fibers (Division of Beaunit Corp.) | Bembella | rayon | A |
| | Bemberg | rayon | A, HF |
| | Comiso | rayon | A, HF |
| | Cupioni | rayon | A, HF |
| | Cupracolor | rayon | A, HF |
| | Cuprel | textured rayon | A, HF |
| | Cuprussah | rayon | A, HF |
| | Dream Slub | nubby rayon | A, HF |
| | Flaikona | rayon | HF |
| | Hi-Narco | rayon | A, HF |
| | Multi-Strata | rayon | A, HF |
| | Narco | rayon | A, HF |

| Company | Fiber | Type | Uses |
|---------|-------|------|------|
| Beaunit Fibers | Narcon | rayon | HF |
| | Nub-Lite | rayon | A, HF |
| | Ondelette | rayon | A, HF |
| | Parfe | rayon | HF |
| | Puff Stuff | polyester | HF |
| | Strata | rayon | HF |
| | Super Stuff | polyester | A, HF |
| | Suprenka | rayon | A, HF |
| | Tough Stuff | polyester | A, HF |
| | Vycron | polyester | A, C, HF |
| Celanese Fibers Co. | Arnel | triacetate | A, HF |
| | Celabond | bonded fabrics | A |
| | Celacloud | acetate fiberfill | A, HF |
| | Celafil | acetate fiberfill | HF |
| | Celaperm | solution-dyed acetate | A, HF |
| | Celara | knit fabrics of textured acetate | A |
| | Celustra | jersey fabric of triacetate yarn | A |
| | Chifonese | acetate curtain cloth | HF |
| | Clairanese | acetate drapery cloth | HF |
| | Multicord | acetate curtain cloth | HF |
| | Permanese | acetate curtain cloth | HF |
| | Prospector | triacetate sharkskin | A |
| | Starset | acetate fabric | A |
| | Tricocel | acetate tricot | A |
| Courtaulds N.A. | Coloray | solution-dyed rayon | A, HF |
| | Fibro | rayon staple | A, C, HF |
| | Shareen | nylon 6 | A, C, HF |
| | Vincell R | modified rayon | A, C, HF |
| | (*) | acrylic | A, C, HF |
| | (*) | acetate | A, C, HF |
| Dow Badische Co. | Anavor | polyester | A, C, HF |
| | Lurex | metallic | A, C, HF |
| | Vivana | nylon 6 | A, C, HF |
| | Zefkrome | solution-dyed acrylic | A, HF |

(*) imported only, no U.S. production

| Company | Fiber | Type | Uses |
|---------|-------|------|------|
| Dow | Zefran | acrylic | A, C, |
| Badische Co. | Zefstat | anti-static yarn | C |
| Du Pont | Acele | acetate | A, HF |
| | Antron | trilobal nylon | A, C, HF |
| | Cantrece | bicomponent nylon | A |
| | Cordura | nylon | I |
| | Dacron | polyester | A, C, HF, I |
| | Lycra | spandex | A |
| | Nomex | nylon | A, C, HF, I |
| | Nylon | nylon 66 | A, C, HF, I |
| | Orlon | acrylic | A, C, HF |
| | Qiana | nylon | A |
| | Taslan | (texturing process) | |
| Eastman | Chromspun | solution-dyed acetate | A, C, HF |
| Chemical | Estron | acetate | A, C, HF |
| Products | Kodel | polyester | A, C, HF |
| Inc. | Verel | modacrylic | A, C, HF |
| Enjay | Enjay mono- | | |
| Fibers & | filament | | |
| Laminates | yarn and | | |
| (Division | ribbon | | |
| of Enjay | fabrics | olefin | C, I |
| Chemicals) | Nylon | tapered nylon | I |
| | Vectra | olefin | C, HF, I |
| Fiber In- | Cedilla | nylon | A |
| dustries | Fortrel | polyester | A, C, HF, I |
| Inc. | Fortrel | | |
| (Jointly | Fiberfill | polyester | A, HF |
| owned by | Fortrel 7 | polyester | A, HF |
| Celanese | Nylon | nylon 66 | A |
| Corp. and | Recall | nylon | A |
| Imperial | | | |
| Chemical | | | |
| Industries | | | |
| Ltd.) | | | |
| Firestone | Nytelle | nylon 6 | A |
| Synthetic | Firestone | | |
| Fibers Co. | Nylon | nylon 6 | I |

| Company | Fiber | Type | Uses |
|---------|-------|------|------|
| Globe Manufac- turing Co. | Globe Rubber | rubber | A, I |
| | Glospan | spandex | A, I |
| Hercules Inc. | Herculon | olefin | A, C, HF, I |
| Hystron | Danufil* | rayon | A, HF |
| | Dolan* | acrylic | A, HF |
| | Star | pentalobal polyester | A |
| | Trevira | polyester | A, C |
| Monsanto Textiles | Acrilan | acrylic | A, C, HF |
| | Astrograf | artificial turf | I |
| | Astroturf | artificial turf | I |
| | Blue C Nylon | nylon 66 | A, HF, I |
| | Blue C Polyester | polyester | A, C, HF, I |
| | Cadon | anti-static nylon | C |
| | Cerex | spunbonded material | A, I, |
| | Chemback | carpet backing | C |
| | Cumuloft | textured nylon | C |
| | Durette | fireproof material | I |
| | Elura | modacrylic | (wigs) |
| | Glace | filament acrylic | A |
| | 22N | anti-stat nylon | A |
| | WD 2 | soil-resistant polyester | A, C |
| Phillips Fibers | Marvess | olefin | C, HF, I |
| | Phillips 66 | nylon 66 | A, C |
| | Quintess | polyester | A, HF |
| UniRoyal | Polycrest | olefin | C |

*no U.S. production . . . fiber produced in West Germany.

# U.S. Man-Made Fiber Production in 1970

## PART NINE

## IN MILLIONS OF POUNDS

| Producer | Rayon | Nylon | Polyester | Acetate | Acrylic | Modacrylic | Olefin |
|---|---|---|---|---|---|---|---|
| Allied Chemical | | 200 | (a) | | | | |
| American Cyanamid | | | 25(b) | | 100 | | |
| American Enka | | 90 | 60 | | | | |
| American Viscose (Division of FMC) | 660 | | 150 | | | | |
| Beaunit Fibers | 140 | 60 | 70 | 60 | | | |
| Celanese | | | | 275(c) | | | |
| Courtaulds N.A. | 200 | 20 | 30 | | 50 | | |
| Dow Badische | | 55 | | 50 | 40 | | |
| Du Pont | | 600 | 475 | 55 | 200 | | |
| Eastman Chemical Products | | | 380 | | | 25 | |
| Enjay Fibers (Div. of Enjay Chemical) | | 25(g) | | | | | 20 |
| Fiber Industries | | 60 | 450 | | | | |
| Firestone Fibers | | 45 | P.P. | | | | |
| Hercules Inc. | | | | | | | 85 |
| Hystron Inc. | | | 100(d) | | (e) | | |
| Monsanto Textiles | | 335 | 85 | | 301 | | |
| Phillips Fibers | | 60 | 20 | | | | 60 |
| UniRoyal | | | | | | | 3(f) |

All data based on Fairchild Publications estimates.
a  80-million pound plant scheduled for start-up in 1971
b  IRC Fibers Co. Subsidiary of American Cyanamid
c  includes triacetate
d  140 million projected for 1972
e  Dolan acrylic and Danufil rayon produced in West Germany by Farbwerke Hoechst
f  rated capacity 25 million
g  monofilament

# Key Industry Statistics

## PART TEN

## A. U.S. MAN-MADE FIBER OUTPUT*
### 1960–1969
*(Millions of Pounds)*

| Year | Rayon & Acetate | Non-Cellulosic | Total |
|------|-----------------|----------------|-------|
| 1969 | 1,576.2 | 3,485.6 | 5,061.8 |
| 1968 | 1,594.3 | 3,212.5 | 4,806.8 |
| 1967 | 1,388.1 | 2,338.2 | 3,726.3 |
| 1966 | 1,519.0 | 2,068.7 | 3,587.7 |
| 1965 | 1,527.0 | 1,776.9 | 3,303.9 |
| 1964 | 1,431.8 | 1,406.5 | 2,838.3 |
| 1963 | 1,348.8 | 1,156.0 | 2,504.8 |
| 1962 | 1,272.1 | 972.9 | 2,245.0 |
| 1961 | 1,095.2 | 750.9 | 1,846.1 |
| 1960 | 1,028.5 | 677.2 | 1,705.7 |

* Not including glass fiber
*Source:* Textile Organon


## B. WORLD MAN-MADE FIBER OUTPUT
### 1960–1969
*(Millions of Pounds)*

| Year | Rayon & Acetate | Non-Cellulosic | Total |
|------|-----------------|----------------|-------|
| 1969 | 7,893 | 9,621 | 17,514 |
| 1968 | 7,783 | 8,320 | 16,103 |
| 1967 | 7,312 | 6,329 | 13,641 |
| 1966 | 7,370 | 5,473 | 12,843 |
| 1965 | 7,360 | 4,521 | 11,881 |
| 1964 | 7,245 | 3,727 | 10,972 |
| 1963 | 6,744 | 2,942 | 9,686 |
| 1962 | 6,315 | 2,382 | 8,697 |
| 1961 | 5,930 | 1,831 | 7,761 |
| 1960 | 5,749 | 1,548 | 7,297 |

*Source:* Textile Organon

## C. U.S. SPUN-YARN PRODUCTION BY TYPE OF SPINNING SYSTEM BY TYPE OF YARN, AND BY END USE: 1968

*(Thousands of pounds)*

| System of spinning | Spun-yarn production, total | Spun yarn classified by principal fiber | | | | |
|---|---|---|---|---|---|---|
| | | Cotton | Wool | Rayon and/or acetate | Non-cellulosic fibers | Other natural fibers: sisal, hemp, jute, etc. |
| Production, all systems total | 6,330,204 | 3,732,276 | 411,396 | 647,267 | 1,363,137 | 176,128 |
| Cotton system, total | 5,250,273 | 3,731,396 | 2,706 | 563,907 | 942,537 | 9,727 |
| Weaving, except carpet | 4,142,742 | 2,932,519 | 1,836 | 460,482 | 738,269 | 9,636 |
| Machine knitting, except carpet | 780,998 | 611,333 | 870 | 27,868 | 140,927 | — |
| Hand knitting | (b) | — | — | — | (b) | — |
| Carpet and rugs | 145,704 | 28,819 | — | 62,904 | 53,981 | (a) |
| Cordage and twine | 49,979 | 49,234 | — | — | (b) | — |
| Tufting, except carpet | 20,541 | 14,101 | — | 6,152 | (a) | — |
| Sewing thread | 76,499 | 69,502 | — | — | 6,997 | — |
| All other uses | (d) | 25,888 | — | 6,501 | (b) | (a) |
| Woolen system, total | 582,723 | 880 | 291,284 | 26,331 | 258,247 | 5,981 |
| Weaving, except carpet | 241,269 | 652 | 165,536 | 18,992 | 51,067 | 5,022 |
| Machine knitting, except carpet | 36,668 | (a) | 23,808 | (a) | 12,360 | (a) |
| Hand knitting | (d) | — | (a) | (c) | (b) | — |
| Carpet and rugs | 299,452 | — | 101,794 | (d) | 191,624 | (b) |
| Cordage and twine | (b) | — | — | — | (b) | — |
| Tufting, except carpet | — | — | — | — | — | — |
| Sewing thread | — | — | — | — | — | — |
| All other uses | 1,947 | (a) | — | (a) | 1,805 | — |

| | | | | | |
|---|---|---|---|---|---|
| Worsted system, total | 342,289 | — | 117,406 | 53,140 | 152,404 | 19,339 |
| Weaving, except carpet | 106,973 | — | 46,771 | 15,204 | 39,271 | 5,727 |
| Machine knitting, except carpet | 130,036 | — | 53,778 | (a) | 75,068 | 1,137 |
| Hand knitting | 19,112 | — | 16,857 | (a) | 2,180 | — |
| Carpet and rugs | 81,063 | — | — | (d) | 35,772 | (d) |
| Cordage and twine | (d) | — | — | — | (a) | (d) |
| Tufting, except carpet | — | — | — | — | — | — |
| Sewing thread | — | — | — | — | — | — |
| All other uses | (a) | — | — | — | (a) | — |
| Other systems, total | 154,919 | — | — | 3,889 | 9,949 | 141,081 |
| Weaving, except carpet | 23,970 | — | — | 3,889 | — | 20,081 |
| Machine knitting, except carpet | (a) | — | — | — | (a) | — |
| Hand knitting | — | — | — | — | — | — |
| Carpet and rugs | 12,486 | — | — | — | (a) | (d) |
| Cordage and twine | 109,521 | — | — | — | (d) | (d) |
| Tufting, except carpet | — | — | — | — | — | — |
| Sewing thread | (a) | — | — | — | — | (a) |
| All other uses | 8,445 | — | — | — | — | 8,445 |

*Note:* In order to avoid disclosure of individual company information, a number of figures have been withheld. In such cases, a letter symbol has been substituted, as follows, to indicate the approximate magnitude of the withheld information.

(a)  Under 500,000 pounds
(b)  500,000 to 999,000 pounds
(c)  1,000,000 to 2,499,000 pounds
(d)  2,500,000 pounds and over
—    Represents zero

## D. SPUN-YARN PRODUCTION BY GEOGRAPHIC AREAS: 1968
### (Thousands of pounds)

| Geographic area | Total | Cotton including blends | Wool and wool blends including reused and re-processed | Spun rayon and/or acetate, including blends | Spun acrylic yarns, including blends | Spun polyester blends with cotton | Spun polyester blends with fibers except cotton | Spun non-cellulosic yarns except acrylic and polyester blends | Other natural fibers |
|---|---|---|---|---|---|---|---|---|---|
| United States, total | 6,330,204 | 3,732,276 | 411,396 | 647,267 | 388,266 | 625,235 | 133,984 | 215,652 | 176,128 |
| New England | 313,076 | 75,582 | 142,357 | 19,286 | 31,893 | 9,910 | 1,374 | 20,395 | 12,279 |
| Maine | 97,301 | 45,422 | 37,223 | 5,173 | 1,508 | (d) | (a) | 4,571 | (a) |
| New Hampshire | 51,133 | (d) | 21,631 | 10,042 | 4,194 | — | (a) | 1,729 | (c) |
| Vermont | (c) | — | (c) | — | — | — | — | — | — |
| Massachusetts | 103,803 | (d) | 48,095 | 2,917 | 17,301 | (d) | 872 | 1,091 | 10,503 |
| Rhode Island | 30,222 | (a) | 26,388 | (a) | 3,516 | (b) | — | (a) | — |
| Connecticut | (d) | (c) | (d) | (c) | 5,374 | — | — | (d) | — |
| Middle Atlantic | 144,394 | (a) | 40,813 | 9,014 | 21,679 | (d) | — | 20,523 | 43,699 |
| New York | 43,192 | (a) | (d) | (c) | 10,510 | — | — | (d) | (d) |
| New Jersey | 22,478 | — | (a) | (a) | (b) | (d) | — | (c) | (d) |
| Pennsylvania | 78,724 | (a) | 29,285 | 7,796 | (d) | — | — | 11,505 | 19,589 |
| East North Central | 24,181 | (b) | 11,584 | (a) | (b) | — | (b) | (c) | 9,705 |
| Ohio | 10,095 | — | 3,514 | — | — | — | — | (b) | (d) |
| Illinois | 7,901 | (b) | (d) | (a) | — | — | (a) | — | (d) |
| Michigan | 688 | (a) | (a) | — | (a) | — | — | (b) | — |
| Wisconsin | 5,497 | — | 4,491 | (a) | (b) | — | (a) | (a) | — |

| | Col 1 | Col 2 | Col 3 | Col 4 | Col 5 | Col 6 | Col 7 | Col 8 | Col 9 |
|---|---|---|---|---|---|---|---|---|---|
| West North Central | 12,935 | — | 2,623 | — | (a) | — | (a) | (c) | 24,803 |
| Minnesota | 1,982 | — | (c) | — | (a) | — | — | — | — |
| Iowa | (a) | — | (a) | — | — | — | — | — | — |
| Missouri | 10,520 | — | (a) | — | — | — | — | (c) | (d) |
| Nebraska | (a) | — | (a) | — | — | — | — | — | — |
| South Atlantic | 4,865,993 | 2,979,887 | 191,094 | 582,050 | 272,126 | 547,075 | 129,513 | 139,445 | (d) |
| Maryland | 8,812 | — | (c) | (d) | (a) | — | (a) | (a) | — |
| Virginia | 145,230 | 50,803 | 30,304 | (d) | (d) | (d) | (d) | (d) | — |
| West Virginia | 1,575 | — | (c) | — | — | — | — | (a) | (a) |
| North Carolina | 1,930,973 | 1,131,397 | 62,477 | 257,731 | 152,569 | 194,266 | 63,440 | 52,492 | 16,601 |
| South Carolina | 1,688,449 | 1,078,104 | 49,758 | 205,016 | 48,814 | 226,351 | (d) | 22,901 | (d) |
| Georgia | 1,090,954 | 719,583 | 45,717 | 109,395 | 65,796 | (d) | 7,252 | 58,570 | (d) |
| East South Central | 811,341 | 590,248 | 17,955 | 34,322 | 59,876 | 57,847 | 1,353 | 19,525 | 30,215 |
| Kentucky | 6,794 | (d) | — | (c) | — | (d) | — | (a) | — |
| Tennessee | 169,126 | 98,766 | 12,503 | (d) | 38,538 | — | — | 11,023 | — |
| Alabama | 583,307 | 469,529 | (d) | 26,457 | (d) | (d) | 1,353 | 7,744 | (c) |
| Mississippi | 52,114 | (d) | (c) | (a) | (d) | (d) | — | (b) | (d) |
| West South Central | 149,385 | 84,779 | (b) | (d) | (c) | (c) | (c) | 42,730 | (d) |
| Arkansas | 33,053 | (d) | — | (b) | — | (a) | (c) | (d) | (d) |
| Louisiana | (d) | — | (b) | — | (c) | — | — | (d) | (d) |
| Texas | (d) | (d) | — | (c) | (c) | (c) | — | (a) | (a) |
| West | 8,899 | (b) | (d) | (d) | (a) | — | — | — | (d) |
| Utah | (a) | — | (a) | — | — | — | — | — | — |
| Washington | (c) | — | (c) | — | (a) | — | — | — | — |
| Oregon | 2,411 | — | (c) | — | (a) | — | — | — | — |
| California | 4,306 | (b) | — | — | — | — | — | — | (d) |

Note: In order to avoid disclosure of individual company information, a number of figures have been withheld. In such cases, a letter symbol has been substituted, as follows, to indicate the approximate magnitude of the withheld information.

(a) Under 500,000 pounds
(b) 500,000 to 999,000 pounds
(c) 1,000,000 to 2,499,000 pounds
(d) 2,500,000 pounds and over
— Represents zero

E. PRODUCTION OF TEXTURED, CRIMPED, OR BULKED FILAMENT YARNS, BY END USE, FIBER, AND METHOD OF DISTRIBUTION: 1968 AND 1967

(Thousands of pounds)

| End use and fiber | 1968 | | | | 1967ʳ | | | |
|---|---|---|---|---|---|---|---|---|
| | Total | For sale | For own use | On commission | Total | For sale | For own use | On commission |
| Textured, crimped, or bulked filament yarns, total | 508,236 | 464,129 | 27,766 | 16,341 | 420,587 | 384,938 | 24,459 | 11,190 |
| Nylon | 408,784 | 379,711 | 13,111 | 15,962 | 315,093 | 294,544 | 9,781 | 10,768 |
| Rayon and acetate | 30,346 | 27,500 | 2,799 | 47 | 30,111 | 26,383 | 3,459 | 269 |
| Other | 69,106 | 56,918 | 11,856 | 332 | 75,383 | 64,011 | 11,219 | 153 |
| Weaving yarn, except carpet, total | 37,140 | (d) | 20,273 | (c) | 34,815 | (d) | 20,518 | (c) |
| Nylon | 17,104 | (d) | (d) | (c) | 15,050 | (d) | (d) | (c) |
| Rayon and acetate | 8,136 | (d) | (c) | — | 8,243 | (d) | (d) | — |
| Other | 11,900 | (c) | 10,431 | (a) | 11,522 | (c) | 10,496 | (a) |
| Knitting yarn, except carpet, total | 167,484 | 155,512 | 6,479 | 5,493 | 126,299 | 117,413 | 3,413 | 5,473 |
| Nylon | 123,758 | 113,907 | 4,705 | 5,146 | 90,726 | 83,091 | 2,584 | 5,051 |
| Rayon and acetate | 19,720 | (d) | (a) | (a) | 19,944 | (d) | (a) | (a) |
| Other | 24,006 | (d) | (c) | (a) | 15,629 | (d) | (b) | (a) |
| Carpet and rug yarns, total | 302,398 | (d) | — | (d) | 258,492 | (d) | — | (d) |
| Nylon | 266,916 | (d) | — | (d) | 208,758 | (d) | — | (d) |
| Rayon and acetate | (c) | (c) | — | — | (c) | (c) | — | — |
| Other | (d) | (d) | — | — | (d) | (d) | — | — |

| | | | | | | | |
|---|---|---|---|---|---|---|---|
| All other uses | 1,124 | (a) | (c) | (a) | 981 | (a) | (b) | — |
| Nylon | 1,006 | (a) | (b) | — | 559 | (a) | (a) | — |
| Rayon and acetate | (a) | (a) | (a) | (a) | (a) | — | (a) | — |
| Other | (a) | (a) | — | — | (a) | (a) | — | — |

*Note:* In order to avoid disclosure of individual company information, a number of figures have been withheld. In such cases, a letter symbol has been substituted, as follows, to indicate the approximate magnitude of the withheld information.

(a) Under 500,000 pounds
(b) 500,000 to 999,000 pounds
(c) 1,000,000 to 2,499,000 pounds
(d) 2,500,000 pounds and over
— Represents zero
r Revised.

F. SPUN-YARN PRODUCTION BY FIBER AND METHOD OF DISTRIBUTION: 1968 AND 1967

*(Thousands of pounds)*

| Type of yarn | 1968 | | | | 1967ʳ | | | |
|---|---|---|---|---|---|---|---|---|
| | Total | For sale | For own use | On commission | Total | For sale | For own use | On commission |
| Spun-yarn production total | 6,330,204 | 1,631,598 | 4,651,087 | 47,519 | 6,323,603 | 1,489,020 | 4,799,345 | 35,238 |
| Cotton | 3,732,276 | 871,038 | 2,858,102 | 3,136 | 4,138,165 | 871,664 | 3,264,358 | 2,143 |
| Wool, including reused and reprocessed wool | 411,396 | 130,998 | 255,863 | 24,535 | 413,146 | 117,210 | 270,731 | 25,205 |
| Rayon and/or acetate | 647,267 | 219,907 | 425,836 | 1,524 | 576,245 | 182,831 | 392,447 | 967 |
| Noncellulosic fibers | 1,363,137 | 369,997 | 975,692 | 17,448 | 1,003,679 | 279,794 | 717,841 | 6,044 |
| Other natural fibers (sisal, hemp, jute, etc.) | 176,128 | 39,658 | 135,594 | 876 | 192,368 | 37,521 | 153,968 | 879 |

ʳ Revised.

184

| G. RAW SILK DELIVERIES* 1960–1969 | | H. RAW COTTON CONSUMPTION 1960–1969 | |
| --- | --- | --- | --- |
| Year | Bales | Year | Bales |
| 1969 | 16,484 | 1969 | 8,298,000 |
| 1968 | 17,049 | 1968 | 8,568,000 |
| 1967 | 19,871 | 1967 | 9,215,000 |
| 1966 | 27,880 | 1966 | 9,647,000 |
| 1965 | 33,190 | 1965 | 9,296,000 |
| 1964 | 36,547 | 1964 | 8,940,000 |
| 1963 | 32,572 | 1963 | 8,394,000 |
| 1962 | 44,926 | 1962 | 8,716,000 |
| 1961 | 48,559 | 1961 | 8,524,000 |
| 1960 | 48,806 | 1960 | 8,706,000 |

* includes small amounts of re-exports

*Source:* Textile Organon

# I. FIBER CONSUMPTION PATTERNS

## U.S. Mill Consumption of Fibers
### (in thousands of pounds)

|                  | 1954      | 1958      | 1964      | 1967       | 1968       |
|------------------|-----------|-----------|-----------|------------|------------|
| Man-Made Fibers  | 1,453,600 | 1,525,400 | 2,953,500 | 3,721,800  | 4,781,800  |
| All Fibers       | 6,028,200 | 5,938,000 | 7,782,800 | 13,578,000 | 16,066,000 |

## Annual per Capita Consumption (in pounds)

|                            | 1954  | 1958  | 1964  | 1967  | 1968  | 10 year % change |
|----------------------------|-------|-------|-------|-------|-------|------------------|
| Man-Made Fibers            | 8.4   | 9.1   | 14.6  | 19.8  | 24.7  | +171.4           |
| All Fibers                 | 35.2  | 33.3  | 40.9  | 46.9  | 50.9  | + 52.9           |
| Population (in millions)   | 163.0 | 174.0 | 192.0 | 199.1 | 201.2 | + 15.0           |

## End-Use Consumption of Man-Made Fibers (in pounds)

|                                                      | 1962        | 1963        | 1967          | 1968*         |
|------------------------------------------------------|-------------|-------------|---------------|---------------|
| Men's & Boys' Wear                                   | 242,300,000 | 260,000,000 | 566,300,000   | 675,200,000   |
| Women's, Missses', Children's, & Infants' Wear       | 567,100,000 | 616,000,000 | 998,000,000   | 1,167,300,000 |
| Home Furnishings                                     | 631,700,000 | 733,000,000 | 1,252,500,000 | 1,569,800,000 |
| Other Consumer-Type Products                         | 289,300,000 | 280,000,000 | 501,000,000   | 572,500,000   |
| Industrial Uses                                      | 661,000,000 | 663,000,000 | 940,800,000   | 1,210,700,000 |

\* Latest Available Data

*Source:* Man-Made Fiber Producers Association Fact Book

## 1. IMPORTS OF COTTON AND MAN-MADE TEXTILES
### 1965 through 1969
*(Figures are in millions)*

| Year | Cottons | | Man-mades | |
|------|---------|-------|-----------|-------|
| | Square yards | Value | Square yards | Value |
| 1969 | 643.7 | $173.5 | 226.4 | $112.4 |
| 1968 | 577.1 | 146.1 | 199.8 | 86.0 |
| 1967 | 543.1* | 138.4 | 175.5** | 63.9 |
| 1966 | 610.6* | 156.7 | 253.0** | 71.5 |
| 1965 | 534.3* | 133.7 | 158.4** | 51.6 |

## 2. EXPORTS OF COTTON AND MAN-MADE TEXTILES
### 1965 through 1969
*(Figures are in millions)*

| Year | Cottons | | Man-mades | |
|------|---------|-------|-----------|-------|
| | Square yards | Value | Square Yards | Value |
| 1969 | 320.8 | $110.7 | 171.0 | $111.1 |
| 1968 | 885.7 | 100.6 | 153.5 | 101.0 |
| 1967 | 312.3 | 108.3 | 161.4 | 108.4 |
| 1966 | 355.0 | 118.2 | 158.5 | 108.3 |
| 1965 | 315.7 | 107.6 | 154.1 | 106.2 |

*Note:* Census data does not include quantity imported for the years 1965, 1966, 1967, in these classes:

\* Fabrics, woven, cotton, n.e.s., not bleached or colored.
\*\* Fabrics, woven, man-made, n.e.s., except pile or chenille.

*Source:* Fairchild Publications Market Research Department based on U.S. Bureau of the Census data.

## 3.  U.S. IMPORTS OF MAN-MADE FIBERS
### *(Figures are in Millions)*

In 1969, the imports of man-made fibers into the United States totalled 231,337,000 pounds. (This figure includes monofilaments, filament yarns, staple, tow, waste and spun yarns.) Although such imports were less than the volume imported in 1968, it is 211% higher than the volume of man-made fibers imported in 1960.

### U. S. Imports—Man-Made Fibers
*(Pounds)*

| Year | Cellulosic | Non-Cellulosic | Total |
|------|-----------|----------------|-------|
| 1960 | 64.6 | 9.7 | 74.3 |
| 1965 | 85.2 | 75.0 | 160.3 |
| 1966 | 120.9 | 95.6 | 216.6 |
| 1967 | 94.8 | 109.5 | 204.4 |
| 1968 | 141.5 | 169.1 | 310.7 |
| 1969 | 97.0 | 134.3 | 231.3 |

## 4.  U.S. IMPORTS OF PRODUCTS CONTAINING MAN-MADE FIBERS
### *(Figures are in Millions)*

The fiber content of imports of fabrics and other articles containing man-made fibers imported in 1969 increased 620% over the average volume imported during the years 1960 through 1964 and was 37% higher than the volume of such imports in 1968.

### U. S. Imports of Products Containing Man-Made Fibers
*(Pounds)*

| Commodity | Yearly Average 1960–1964 | 1965 | 1966 | 1967 | 1968 | 1969 |
|-----------|--------------------------|------|------|------|------|------|
| Cloth | 15.3 | 33.7 | 51.7 | 41.2 | 48.0 | 60.8 |
| Wearing Apparel | 11.2 | 30.8 | 38.6 | 61.1 | 91.5 | 144.1 |
| Industrial | .3 | .6 | 1.8 | 1.0 | 5.3 | 3.4 |
| All Other | 6.6 | 12.7 | 26.4 | 26.5 | 30.2 | 32.3 |
| Total | 33.4 | 77.8 | 118.5 | 129.8 | 175.0 | 240.6 |

*Source:* Man-Made Fiber Producers Association

## K.  SHARE OF WORLD MARKET BY COUNTRY

**Producing Capacity, Production, Imports, and Exports**

The following charts and supporting data show the relative positions of EEC (European Economic Community: Belgium/Luxembourg, France, Italy, Netherlands, and West Germany); EFTA (European Free Trade Association: Austria, Denmark, Norway, Portugal, Sweden, Switzerland, and the United Kingdom); Japan; and the United States with respect to producing capacity, production, exports, and imports of man-made fibers in 1968.

The figures present only data on yarn, staple fiber, and tow for textile uses.

Although in comparison with EEC, EFTA, and Japan, the United States' share of capacity in 1968 was almost 40% of the total, and production was almost 40% of the total, the United States' share of exports was less than 7% of the total.

| **Producing Capacity** | | | **Production** | | |
|---|---|---|---|---|---|
| | **Millions of Pounds** | **%** | | **Millions of Pounds** | **%** |
| EEC | 3,989.6 | 27.7 | EEC | 3,135.5 | 25.8 |
| EFTA | 1,894.4 | 13.1 | EFTA | 1,659.4 | 13.6 |
| JAPAN | 2,833.5 | 19.7 | JAPAN | 2,590.7 | 21.3 |
| U.S. | 5,694.5 | 39.5 | U.S. | 4,781.8 | 39.3 |
| | 13,881.5 | 100.0 | | 12,167.4 | 100.0 |

| **Imports** | | | **Exports** | | |
|---|---|---|---|---|---|
| | **Millions of Pounds** | **%** | | **Millions of Pounds** | **%** |
| EEC | 841.6 | 53.6 | EEC | 1,659.5 | 53.5 |
| EFTA | 455.2 | 28.9 | EFTA | 707.7 | 22.8 |
| JAPAN | 2.2 | 0.1 | JAPAN | 534.6 | 17.3 |
| U.S. | 273.7 | 17.4 | U.S. | 197.4 | 6.4 |
| | 1,572.7 | 100.0 | | 3,099.2 | 100.0 |

*Source:* Man-Made Fiber Producers Association

## L. SOME PHYSICAL PROPERTIES OF MAN-MADE FIBERS

*(Standard laboratory conditions for fiber tests: 70° F and 65% relative humidity)*

| Fiber | Breaking Tenacity[1] (grams per denier) (standard) | (wet) | Specific Gravity[2] | Standard Moisture Regain[3] (%) | Effects of Heat |
|---|---|---|---|---|---|
| **acetate** (filament and staple) | 1.2 to 1.5 | 0.8 to 1.2 | 1.32 | 6.0 | Sticks at 350 to 375° F. Softens at 400 to 445° F. Melts at 500° F. Burns relatively slowly. |
| **acrylic** (filament and staple) | 2.0 to 3.5 | 1.8 to 3.3 | 1.14 to 1.19 | 1.3 to 2.5 | Sticks at 450 to 497° F., depending on type. |
| **modacrylic** (filament and staple) | 2.0 to 3.5 | 2.0 to 3.5 | 1.30 to 1.37 | .4 to 4 | Will not support combustion. Shrinks at 250°F. Stiffens at temperatures over 300° F. |
| **nylon** nylon 66 (regular-tenacity filament) | 3.0 to 6.0 | 2.6 to 5.4 | 1.14 | 4.0 to 4.5 | Sticks at 445° F. Melts at about 550° F. |
| nylon 66 (high-tenacity filament) | 6.0 to 9.5 | 5.0 to 8.0 | 1.14 | 4.0 to 4.5 | Same as above. |
| nylon 66 (staple) | 3.5 to 7.2 | 3.2 to 6.5 | 1.14 | 4.0 to 4.5 | Same as above. |
| nylon 6 (filament) | 6.0 to 9.5 | 5.0 to 8.0 | 1.14 | 4.5 | Melts at 414 to 428° F. |
| nylon 6 (staple) | 2.5 | 2.0 | 1.14 | 4.5 | Melts at 414 to 428° F. |